BLIGHTY

A PORTRAIT OF CIVILIAN LIFE IN BRITAIN DURING
THE FIRST WORLD WAR, 1914-1918.

BLIGHTY

BY

G. E. DIGGLE

MELKSHAM

COLIN VENTON

WHITE HORSE LIBRARY

ISBN 0 85475 114 9

COPYRIGHT NOTICE

Set 11 on 12 point Intertype Baskervill
and printed in Great Britain
at the Press of the Publisher,
The Uffington Press,
Melksham, Wiltshire,
SN12 6LA (U.K.).

LIST OF CONTENTS

List of Contents (Continued)

LIST OF ILLUSTRATIONS

FOR OLIVE

a third book—with love

Chapter 1

ON THE BRINK

"Tiddley, iddley, ighty! Hurry me back to Blighty.
Blighty is the place for me!"

So sang the troops on active service abroad during the First World
War. The word "Blighty" had been used for many years by the
army in India, and came into general use in the west during the
war of 1914-18. It was a corruption of the Hindustani "bilayati",
meaning foreign, a term used by a foreigner for his native province,
and hence for "home".

Amid the muck and the vermin, the long periods of boredom
interspersed by periods of acute danger, amid the discomforts and
the slaughter, in Flanders and other battlefronts, old England
seemed a most desirable place, almost a Paradise. Living under
such conditions soldiers coveted a "Blighty one", a wound severe
enough to ensure being sent back to England to recuperate.

But was England really such a desirable place to live in during
the second decade of the twentieth century? How did the great
mass of ordinary people fare in the first half of 1914, when un-
realisingly, we stood on the brink of disaster? At the time of writing
there are plenty of old people about who grew up in the opening
decades of this century, and are ready and willing to tell us what
life was like then. But old people's memories are notoriously un-
reliable. The historian must be prepared to check, and to re-check,
from such records as are available, if he is to present a true picture.
Listening to some reminiscences of those legendary times "before
the first war", we get the impression of a Golden Age which came

9

abruptly to an end on 4th August, 1914. People were contented with their lot, and "knew their place"! Anybody who wanted work could have it, and only bone-idle, good-for-nothings were unemployed! Churches and chapels were full every Sunday! Young people showed respect to their elders in a way they no longer do in this degenerate second half of the twentieth century! Writing in 1973, one who grew up in that pre-1914 world stated that, "Strikes and industrial unrest were unknown. The bosses were the bosses, from the Prime Minister to the grocer with one assistant."

Significantly he added, "I have no records to refer to, only an imperfect memory."

When war was declared in 1914 King George V and Queen Mary had entered on the fifth year of their reign. The handsome and charming Prince of Wales, the future Edward VIII, was twenty years of age. His brother, Albert, the future George VI, was eighteen years old, and a midshipman in the Royal Navy. A Liberal government had been in office since 1906. In 1914 Henry Herbert Asquith was Prime Minister, David Lloyd George was Chancellor of the Exchequer, Edward Grey was Secretary of State for Foreign Affairs, and Winston Spencer Churchill was First Lord of the Admiralty. Only recently had certain great Victorians departed from the earthly scene. Florence Nightingale died in 1910, W. S. Gilbert in 1911, General Booth in 1912, and Joseph Chamberlain as recently as 2nd July, 1914. Exponents of the doctrine of inevitable human progress had recently received a severe shock when, in 1912, the so-called unsinkable *Titanic* sank on its maiden voyage. Hindsight proclaimed this as an omen of the approaching end of the unsinkable age of inevitable human progress.

For the 1¼ million income tax payers, and their dependents, there was gracious living in 1914. In parks and suburban avenues nannies escorted well-washed, well-dressed, well-fed children. In the mean streets and alleys, to be found in every town and city, unwashed, ill-fed, raggedly dressed, often lousy children, played on

10

the pavements and in the gutters. Many of them went barefoot, even in winter. Every town and city had its filthy, dilapidated slums.

London had its East End, and provincial centres their equivalent areas of poverty like Manchester's Ancoats and Liverpool's Scotland Road. On Saturday evenings, when "the drink was in", policemen ventured into these districts in pairs, sometimes in threes and fours. The large town houses of the rich had their ground floor drawing and dining rooms, and their first floor family bedrooms, nurseries and bathrooms. The servants slept above these, in the attics, and worked below ground level, in the kitchens, larders and wash houses. Bathrooms had become general among the wealthy and comfortably off, but the less affluent majority made do with a tin bath in front of the kitchen fire. Electricity had generally displaced gas for lighting the big houses, but electric cookers were rare.

In between the minorities of rich and comfortably off (say those who paid income tax) and the very poor, was the great mass of generally respectable, decent, hardworking people, who could have made good use of heavier pay packets. The lowest figure at which income tax was assessed was £160, which meant that six-sevenths of earners escaped. Millions of these good people eked out their scanty wages with a due sense of responsibility. They lived, in the towns, in long rows of identical houses, some of them back to back. Cooking was done on a gas stove, or on a cast iron range, which needed constant polishing with black lead. Country people often lived in picturesque, but insanitary cottages, "two up and two down". Cooking was done on a range or on an oil stove. A garden, and sometimes a pig in the sty, provided extra nourishment. At the end of the garden stood the bucket closet. Water came from the garden well. In town and country the washing of clothes and household linen was done by "tub and scrub". Many a widow eked out a living as a washerwoman to more affluent acquaintances. The rural housewife enjoyed superior drying facilities in her garden, free from the smoke, smuts and grime that penetrated the town housewife's backyard.

Since the Boer War, at the beginning of the century, prices generally had risen. However, with care, a man earning £2 per week or less could obtain the necessities of life for his family. A 4 lb. loaf of bread cost 5d. Milk was 2d. per pint; eggs 1d. each, sometimes a little more, sometimes a little less, according to the season of the year. Digestive rolled oats made a cheap and nourishing breakfast. At 2d. per pound, this worked out at five breakfasts for 1d. Bacon cost 1/- per pound. Meat—mutton or beef—could be bought for round about 6d. per pound. Wild Woodbine cigarettes cost 1d. for five, and beer was 3d. a pint.

In the matter of men's clothing, a flat cloth cap could be bought from 6½d. upwards; a dress shirt in white drill for 3/11d, and a whole suit, made to measure, usually in some dark material, for from 30/- upwards. A young couple, setting up house, could buy items like upholstered wicker chairs for 7/6d each; a hearth-rug for from 1/11d upwards; blankets from 7/6d a pair, and when baby came, a bassinet for 24/-. Terrace houses in a typical industrial town could be rented at 4/-, 5/- or 6/- per week according to the neighbourhood. But at that time the average wage earned by adult women was a mere 10/10½d, and for men £1/5/9d. "Sweated labour" was common in the poorer parts of London and other cities. A woman, hand-finishing a dozen shirts at full speed, could earn 1½d in 45 minutes. Hand-finishing fancy shirts brought 3d. for every dozen completed, but that took over an hour. A man who wanted to "get away from it all" at the weekend could save up for a Raleigh all-steel bicycle at £5/19/6d.

Hair was still woman's crowning glory, masses of it, often surmounted by a large hat loaded with imitation fruit and flowers, and kept in place with long hatpins. The hobble skirt enjoyed a brief period in favour with those who could afford to keep abreast with current fashions. It required but a quarter of the cloth used in an ordinary skirt of the day, and measured barely a yard round the hem. Ladies' stockings were made of wool, cotton or lisle. The era of the silk stocking was still in the future. Men wore flat caps, trilbies or bowlers, and in the summer time flat straw "boaters". Top hats were losing favour, even for Sunday wear. Necks were encased in low, stiff collars, or wing collars, or the increasingly popular soft collar. Boots, rather than shoes, were worn by most men. "Best" or "Sunday" suits and dresses were still in favour.

Leisure hours were much fewer in those days. As a means of cheap amusement the cinema was becoming increasingly popular, and "the pictures" were already being blamed for juvenile delinquency. In a typical northern industrial town the prices of admission to the cinema were 2d., 4d., 6d. and 1/-, though in the poorer parts of the town admission to a "flea pit" or "bug house" cinema was as low as 1d., 2d. and 3d. For these modest sums patrons could enjoy films like *Oliver Twist* (3,300 ft. long); *Sixty Years a Queen* (7,000 ft. long); the latest news items presented by *Pathé Gazette;* a weekly episode of a serial story, like "Lucille Love, the girl of mystery, captured by savages and treated as a goddess"; and sporting events like the Carpentier v. Gunboat Smith fight. When war broke out the Hepworth Company was engaged in making a film of *Barnaby Rudge,* at Walton-on-Thames. The film would last for 83 minutes. No less than a thousand "extras" were employed in the Gordon riots scene, for which each man received 5/- per day, plus cheese and beer.

Many people made their own music. Church and chapel choirs and local choral and operatic societies were well supported. In many northern towns the annual performance of Handel's *Messiah* was one of the great musical events of the year. In the world of instrumental music brass bands were popular, especially in the north. Besses o' t' Barn, Wingate's Temperance, St. Hilda's Colliery, Horwich R.M.I., were some of the best known. In London Sir Henry Wood presided over his Queen's Hall Promenade concerts, with a young man called Adrian Boult as his assistant. In those pre-BBC days it is doubtful whether more than 50,000 people in all England had heard a symphony performed by a full orchestra. In the home the more affluent held musical evenings at which local vocalists sang songs like *Sweet*

13

Genevieve or *The Trumpeter,* and a pianist played the *Moonlight Sonata.* In pious circles the family and friends still gathered round the piano or American organ, and sang hymns after church on Sunday evening. By 1914 the gramophone, as Bernard Shaw observed, "for all its wheezing, snarling and braying," was steadily improving its performance. People who had trained themselves to ignore the hissing of the steel needle on the record could enjoy the thread of music audible amid the extraneous noises. As Mr. Shaw observed, this meant that we had now reached a point where, say in some rural backwater, where church music was made by a few well intentioned ladies with the help of a wheezy pipe organ or harmonium, they could hear masses by Palestrina, and discover that Jackson in F, and hymns Ancient and Modern were not the last word in beauty and propriety in the praises of God.

The music hall was a popular form of entertainment, and received royal recognition when King George V requested the first Variety Command Performance, at the Palace Theatre, London, on 1st July, 1912. George Robey, "the Prime Minister of Mirth"; Harry Lauder, with his Scottish songs, Harry Tate, Florrie Ford, Marie Lloyd, and Vesta Tilley were among the great names in the 1914 music hall. In the summer of 1914 the Londoner, or the visitor to London, could be amused at Maskelyn and Devant's Mysteries, at St. George's Hall, in Oxford Circus, and then proceed to the Anglo-American Exposition at the White City, whose attractions included a real Wild West Ranch.

Travel was cheap. A half-day return ticket from Nottingham to London cost 5/-, and a full day's excursion 8/-. A single ticket from Tilbury to Rotterdam, on a new fast steamer, cost 13/-. Further north a day's sail on Macbrayne's Mail Steamer, *Columbia,* from Glasgow, sailing to Dunoon, Rothesay and Oban, via Greenock, cost 7/-, including three meals. Entertainment for the journey was provided by a German band. Trains were fast. The 5.5 a.m. Great Northern Line express from King's Cross, drawn by a 4-4-2 Atlantic class locomotive, was scheduled

14

to reach Edinburgh by 1.32 p.m.

Sport lovers were well catered for. In 1914 King George V attended the Association Cup Final for the first time. At the Crystal Palace ground (Wembley Stadium was not opened until 1923), he saw Burnley defeat Liverpool 1—0. Blackburn Rovers were the League champions that year. The Rugby League Cup winners were Hull Kingston Rovers, who defeated Wakefield Trinity, at Halifax, 6—0. Salford headed the League Table that year. Turning to cricket, Surrey were County Champions. J. W. Hearne headed the batting averages with 2,116 runs, an average of 60.45 per innings. Jack Hobbs, who was second, scored 2,605 runs, an average of 58.63. Colin Blythe headed the bowling averages, with 170 wickets taken at the cost of 15.19 runs per wicket. The all-rounder, F. E. Woolley, scored 2,272 runs and took 125 wickets. In the boxing world Bombardier Billy Wells had been heavyweight champion since 1911, a position he retained throughout the war years until Joe Beckett defeated him in 1919. On the tennis courts women dressed in ankle-length skirts and petticoats, with a blouse fastened to the skirt with safety pins in case of accident. Mrs. Lambert Chambers was the ladies' singles' champion in 1914, and Norman Brooks, of Australia, was men's champion.

The world of industry seethed with discontent. The memory of the great railway strike in 1911, and the dockers' and coal miners' strike in 1912, were still fresh in men's minds. The first half of 1914 averaged 150 strikes per month. When war broke out the Trade Unions were on the point of launching big demands for improvements in wages and conditions. It is true that the years before 1914 had seen the beginnings of the Welfare State. Old Age Pensions were instituted in 1908. Labour Exchanges had been set up all over the country in 1909. The National Insurance Act of 1911 attempted to deal with health and unemployment. After 1911 the government was too preoccupied with the Irish question to spare time for more, and much needed, social measures. Unrest among the workers grew until, on the eve of the outbreak of war the new Triple Alliance of Miners, Railwaymen and Transport workers was preparing for the biggest strike yet known. Ulster was threatening civil war, and the British garrison at Curragh rebelled at the prospect of enforcing Home Rule on Ulster. Suffragettes in England were destroying property wholesale, to assert the rights of women to the vote. They were imprisoned, forcibly fed, released when their health broke down, then as they regained strength, re-imprisoned under the notorious "Cat and Mouse Act". A fierce spirit of revolt was abroad in England in 1914. Millions were anything but contented with their lot.

In spite of the conditions chronicled above there was a general mood of optimism among the Churches. A future Bishop of London, J. W. C. Wand, described those early 20th century years as the heyday of religious observance in the West. Latourette, the great Church historian, described the years 1815-1914, as "The Great Century" when the Church enjoyed a period of worldwide expansion. Although the majority of British people were non-churchgoers many churches and chapels were well filled every Sunday. Nor was it only the suburban churches that attracted large congregations. Men like Canon Peter Green, in the slums of Salford, the Central Halls of Methodism and the Salvation Army citadels all drew the crowds. Since 1903 Dr. Randall Thomas Davidson had been Archbishop of Canterbury. Leading Free Churchmen included Dr. John Clifford, pastor of Westbourne Baptist Church, London; the Wesleyan Dr. J. Scott Lidgett, of Bermondsey; Dr. Dinsdale T. Young, drawing the largest regular congregation in the country at the huge new Wesleyan Central Hall at Westminster; and Bramwell Booth, who had succeeded his father as General of the Salvation Army. The Congregational Rev. Charles Silvester Horne (father of Kenneth Horne, the radio comedian), combined being pastor of Whitefield's Tabernacle, in Tottenham Court Road, with being Member of Parliament (Liberal) for Ipswich. Perhaps not surprisingly, he died suddenly, at the age of 49, on 2nd May, 1914. A

16

few days before his death he expressed himself thus : "Over this world of military camps, bristling frontiers and armoured fleets, there is heard today with new insistence the ever-romantic strains of the angels' song of Peace and Goodwill." He went on to express his belief that "we are on the eve of applications of Christ's teaching which will revive the interests of the people in Christianity to an astonishing degree." As evidence of his great hope he drew attention to the remarkable spread of the Brotherhood Movement in the last few years. Hundreds of thousands of men had been attracted to church premises for Pleasant Sunday Afternoons. In a typical northern industrial town they listened to addresses on such themes as "The Day of the Bottom Dog", "Was Jesus Christ a Socialist?", and "Jesus Christ and Labour". So the people of Britain went on their lawful, and some of them unlawful, occasions, eating and drinking, marrying and giving in marriage, until the flood came and swept multitudes of them away.

Chapter Two

OVER THE BRINK

GOD forbid that we should ever read a headline: 'PRINCE OF WALES ASSASSINATED ON IRISH VISIT.' What a storm of mingled horror and indignation would sweep over Britain in such an event! "They can't get away with this! We must teach these Irish a lasting lesson!", would be the cry. Something like that happened at the end of June, 1914, in far off Bosnia, a part of the ramshackle Austro-Hungarian Empire. On Sunday, 28th June, Archduke Franz Ferdinand, heir to the throne, and his morganatic wife, Sophie, were shot and fatally wounded by the student, Gavrilo Princip, while visiting Sarajevo, the capital of Bosnia. The event caused little stir in Britain. Why should it? But on the continent tension steadily mounted throughout July as statesmen conferred and an Austrian ultimatum to Serbia was followed by Austria's declaration of war on Serbia on Tuesday, 28th July.

Then the British government began to awaken to a sense of danger, though the feeling was shared by very few ordinary citizens. Joseph Rank, the flour millionaire, unconcernedly went ahead with his holiday plans, and took his family to Marienbad, in Austria, during that last week in July. Six weeks later he and his interned family were exchanged for non-military Austrians caught in England by the outbreak of war. One citizen who awoke to the threatened danger was 25-year-old John Reith, later to become the first director-general of the B.B.C. On Wednesday,

18

29th July, he wrote in his diary the word "WAR". As a Territorial officer he had actually been looking forward to war for years, and now it was coming! This feeling of anticipation was an entirely personal affair, with no thought of what it might mean to home, country or civilisation. It was on that day, too, unbeknown to the man-in-the-street, that the First Fleet left to take up battle stations north of Scotland. The sense of impending catastrophe now began to grow among the thinking section of the populace, as well as in military and government circles. Sir Norman Angell, author of the best-selling book about war, *The Great Illusion*, hastily contacted all he thought would be interested to form a Neutrality League. Its object—keep Britain neutral in the event of a European War. This short-lived organisation was born on Thursday evening, 30th July, and expired within the week. The next day, Friday, saw the closing of the Stock Exchange, and the raising of the Bank Rate to 8 per cent.

Then there followed what was perhaps the most hectic, feverish, apprehensive weekend in British history. The next four days were times of mounting tension and uncertainty, accompanied by a dramatic swing of public opinion in favour of war. On Saturday, 1st August, Germany declared war on Russia. The British section of the International Socialist Bureau met on that day, and issued a manifesto signed by Keir Hardie and Arthur Henderson. They forthrightly denounced any attempt to bring Britain into a war on the side of Russia. They called upon all workers to stand firm for peace, and to refuse to allow the government to commit them to war. For Socialists Czarist Russia meant the horrors of Siberia for political offenders. Russia stood for Jewish pogroms, and for the massacre of workers who peacefully petitioned about their low wages and poor working conditions. It was unthinkable that the lives of British working men should be sacrificed to bolster up such a tyranny. On that day, too, the Governor of the Bank of England told Mr. Lloyd George (the Chancellor of the Exchequer), on behalf of the City, that financial and trading interests in the City of London were totally

19

opposed to British intervention in any European War. Meanwhile, the Bank Rate went up to 10 per cent.

Sunday brought further ominous developments. Germany presented an ultimatum to Belgium, demanding a passage for her troops to invade France. The German army, without presenting any ultimatum, invaded the Grand Duchy of Luxemburg. On that Sunday afternoon there was a great anti-war meeting in Trafalgar Square. Keir Hardie, Arthur Henderson and George Lansbury denounced war. A section of the crowd sang *The Red Flag* and the *Internationale*. But the general mood of the vast crowd was one of anxiety, rather than of excitement. The meeting passed a resolution protesting against the threat of war, against the secret diplomacy responsible for war, against support for Russia, and in favour of British neutrality and of maintaining the international solidarity of the working classes. It was observed that Ramsay MacDonald, the leader of the Labour Party, was absent from this meeting. He had been summoned to an important meeting of the Cabinet at 10 Downing Street. At that meeting Mr. Lloyd George declared himself in favour of British neutrality, providing Germany respected the neutrality of Belgium, and provided that German warships did not enter the English Channel to attack French ports and shipping.

Mr. Asquith, the Prime Minister, noted with distaste that day the beginnings of war hysteria. Large crowds gathered in Whitehall, the Mall, and in front of Buckingham Palace, where they cheered the King. They did not finally disperse until 1 a.m. the next morning. Mr. Asquith acidly observed that war, or anything that seems likely to lead to war, had always been popular with the London mob. "How one loathes such levity!" he remarked, recalling Sir Robert Walpole's saying that: "Now they are ringing the bells; in a few weeks they will be wringing their hands."

Meanwhile, in the provinces, others were speaking very forcibly about the prospect of war. That evening the Rev. Dr. A. T. Guttery, a Methodist leader, expressed himself thus, in the Winter Gardens, Blackpool: "Britain is being invited to plunge herself

20

into a fury that is insane. We are urged to wreck our commerce, endanger our Empire, and to abandon all dreams of social progress, that the Slav may conquer the Teuton, and Russia may dominate the continent. It is the policy of Bedlam, and the statecraft of hell. The Christian Churches must plead for peace, and for the neutrality that would make peace possible. To avenge the murder of an Austrian prince by the horrors of a European War is sheer lunacy." His theme was "The Madness of Europe."

So Sunday passed into Monday—August Bank Holiday. Unduly optimistic, would-be holiday makers, assembling at railway stations, discovered that all excursion trains, and some of the ordinary trains, too, had been cancelled. Deprived of their chance of a trip to Southend-on-Sea, Margate, Ramsgate or Brighton, great crowds of young Londoners, congregated in the Mall, in Trafalgar Square and in Whitehall now openly demonstrating for war with Germany. In the afternoon Mr. Asquith and Mr. Lloyd George walked through dense throngs from Downing Street to the House of Commons. The density of the crowd made police assistance necessary for the two statesmen. Asquith described them as "cheering crowds of loafers and holidaymakers." "I have never been a popular character with the man-in-the-street, and all this gave me scant pleasure," he wrote. That afternoon they listened to Sir Edward Grey, the Foreign Secretary, making clear Britain's place and responsibility in the crisis. It was Grey who, in the Foreign Office that day, crashed his fists on the table, crying: "I hate war!" It was that same evening, while watching the lamplighters at work in St. James' Park, that Grey made his oft quoted remark: "The lamps are going out all over Europe. We shall not see them lit again in our lifetime."

As evening drew on the crowds thickened rather than dispersed. Not since Mafeking night had London streets been so thronged with excited crowds.

At 6.45 p.m. Germany declared war on France. Lord Kitchener of Khartoum, home on leave from Egypt, had reached

21

Dover on his intended return to that country, when he was recalled to London by Asquith, on urgent business of state. Britain had sent an ultimatum to Germany stating that unless by midnight, Central European Time (11 p.m. Greenwich Mean Time), assurances were received that Germany would respect the neutrality of Belgium, a state of war would exist between the two nations. Between Saturday and Monday the prospect of war had leapt into popularity, and the reason was the German threat to Belgium.

Tuesday, 4th August, Britain's day of destiny, dawned. The banks remained closed, and continued closed on the 5th and 6th. Shrewd businessmen declared knowingly that, even if war was declared, no nation had money reserves for more than six weeks of modern warfare. The *Manchester Guardian* carried a full page advertisement from the Neutrality League. It was headed: "BRITONS, DO YOUR DUTY AND KEEP YOUR COUNTRY OUT OF A WICKED AND STUPID WAR". Unfortunately, the thousands of young men in straw "boaters" and young women in light calico dresses, who assembled in Parliament Square and Whitehall, were not readers of the *Manchester Guardian*. They sang *Rule, Britannia, Three cheers for the Red, White and Blue,* and even the *Marseillaise,* in the intervals of shouting "Down with Germany!"

Excitement mounted as the day wore on with no reply from Germany. When the House of Commons rose at 4.30 p.m., Mr. Asquith escaped for an hour's solitary motor drive, in order to collect his thoughts and to survey his feelings. In the early evening he returned to Downing Street to join his colleagues in the Cabinet Room, to await the expiration of the ultimatum. They waited, Asquith, Lloyd George, Grey, Haldane and McKenna, in an atmosphere of deep and solemn intensity. All the afternoon crowds massed in front of Buckingham Palace, waiting for news. At 8 p.m. King George, wearing the uniform of an Admiral of the Fleet, Queen Mary, the Prince of Wales and Princess Mary appeared on the balcony of the Palace. The crowd cheered wildly,

22

and sang *For he's a jolly good fellow*. Feeling intensified as the fateful hour of 11 o'clock approached. In the Cabinet Room Lloyd George described the atmosphere as like waiting for a signal to pull a lever that would hurl millions to their deaths— unless a last minute reprieve arrived. When no message came from Germany, and Big Ben struck eleven Mr. Lloyd George felt as if our planet had been snatched from its orbit, and sent spinning into the unknown by some demonic hand. According to Margot, wife of the Prime Minister, the only happy face in 10 Downing Street that night was that of Winston Churchill, First Lord of the Admiralty.

As she made for bed she observed Winston standing towards the double doors of the Cabinet Room, a pleased look on his face, perhaps because he knew that the Fleet was prepared, and that the Committee of Imperial Defence was also ready with plans for just this emergency. But, at that moment neither Winston nor any one else, realised the number of men, the amount of armaments and defence works the now imminent conflict would demand.

Meanwhile, outside Buckingham Palace the news that Britain was now at war was greeted with tremendous cheering, which grew into a positively deafening roar when the King, Queen and the Prince of Wales appeared once again on the Palace balcony. The crowds then decided to "make a night of it". A special force of mounted and unmounted police from Cannon Row had the utmost difficulty in maintaining order in the main thoroughfares around Westminster and Charing Cross. In spite of the best efforts of the police the crowd succeeded in breaking the windows of the German Embassy.

So an era ended, and Britain plunged over the brink into what then came to be known as the Great War, and later as the First World War. "So it's come at last," said the few. As long ago as 1895, Mr. Gladstone, watching the Kaiser's yacht sail through the lines of German battleships at the opening of the Kiel Canal, shrewdly observed, "This means war." Lord Roberts, with his call for conscription years before hostilities broke out, was another true prophet. Sir Edward Marshall Hall, the distinguished advocate, was another who foresaw the coming of war. Having married a German wife, the daughter of a Hamburg ship owner, he had contacts with Germany which gave him some knowledge of the strength of the German war party. In contrast to this the feelings of the many might be expressed in the words : "Whoever would have thought it?" As we have noted many shrewd, hardheaded men of business subscribed to this view. So too did men like the musician, Sir Henry Wood. "It came as a bolt from the blue!" was his reaction. "The outbreak of war came as a great shock," said the Rev. Hewlett Johnson, then a clergyman at Altrincham, and later to become known as the "Red" Dean of Canterbury. The British people were taken by surprise, and they launched themselves into conflict with great cheerfulness and enthusiasm. Never was a war more popular in its beginnings than this one.

Chapter 3

BUSINESS AS USUAL?

NOTE the question mark in the chapter heading. "Business as usual" was our first national war slogan. It was coined by businessmen who hoped to combine profitmaking with duty to King and country. But from the very beginning of the war it became increasingly plain that the nation was faced with the task of a major adjustment to the new situation.

Housewives were at once called upon to adjust their finances to steadily rising prices. An 5th August the price of imported meat rose by 1d. per pound, and the price of a 4 lb. loaf rose from 5d. to 8d. There was a mild stampede to lay in stocks of food against a possible emergency. The government warned against panic buying, and the hoarding of gold. Food distributors generally acted with a sense of responsibility to the public. For instance, in one northern town the grocers conferred, and agreed to stabilise the price of bacon at 1/1d per pound, butter at 1/9d, and sugar at 2 lbs. for 7½d., in their locality. A little later the government raised tea duty from 5d. to 8d. per pound, and the duty on a barrel of beer from 7/9d to 25/-. Gold sovereigns were replaced by notes to the value of £1 and 10/-. £3 million worth of notes were available by 7th August, and £5 million a day after that. By the end of 1914 the housewife had been called upon to adapt her housekeeping allowance to a 20 per cent rise in the cost of living.

Business as usual? How could that be when thousands of young men, eager for an escape from the dull, drab, daily routine of shop, factory and office life, were flocking to join the armed forces? If the optimists were right, and the war would be over by Christmas, then the business life of the country might have been carried on with relatively little disturbance. But the newly-appointed Secretary of State for War, Earl Horatio Herbert Kitchener of Khartoum and of Broome foresaw a long war. He was convinced of the need for conscription, but deferred to Asquith's view that this was not then politically expedient. Instead he took immediate steps to raise a large volunteer army. His first appeal was for 100,000 men, aged between 19 and 30, to serve for three years, or for the duration of the war. This first appeal was limited to 100,000 because of the difficulty of equipping them. This first 100,000 enlisted, an appeal for a second 100,000 was launched on 28th August. So the appeals continued until by mid-November 700,000 men had enlisted.

The recruitment campaigns were greatly helped by a striking poster, by Alfred Leete, which appeared on hoardings everywhere. It portrayed Kitchener's face, with glaring eyes, heavy moustache, and pointing finger. Under the portrait was the slogan : "Your King and Country need YOU." On one of these posters someone scribbled a pertinent enquiry :

> Your King and Country need you,
> You hardy sons of toil,
> But will your King and Country need you
> When they're sharing out the spoil?

However, in the general and unprecedented upsurge of patriotism, few thought to ask such questions. Hundreds of thousands of young men began the task of adjustment from a commercial or industrial, to a military regime. Journalists and other writers played a large part in helping the civilian, and the military, population to adjust to the new circumstances. As this was before the day of radio and television the householder relied upon the morning and evening newspapers, and upon the special editions thereof, to keep him abreast of events. During the first few tense weeks news was understandably scarce. The French armies hurried to take up their battle positions, and the British Expeditionary Force hastened to embark for France. Over the breakfast table, and on the morning and evening businessmen's trains, news columns were eagerly scanned. The first definite news of actual fighting came from Alsace-Lorraine, the district taken by the Germans from the French in 1871.

ALSACE INVADED! FRENCH DASH OVER THE FRONTIER reported the London *Times,* when the war was a week old. Two days later the French mastery of Alsace was announced. By 17th August the British public was thrilled to read of the Germans being driven from Dunant, and that the French had captured a fortress in Lorraine. Better news still came on 18th August. The British Expeditionary Force was safely across the Channel, without the loss of a single soldier from enemy action. Now let the so-called invincible German army beware! They had invaded Belgium, but it was not yet clear whether they had managed to get past the fortresses of Liège. Even if they did so, well, there was a place called Waterloo in Belgium. How appropriate if, after almost a century, another tyrant met his defeat at the hands of the British, aided by the French and the Belgians of course, at the place called Waterloo! Then bad news began to pour in. On 21st August *The Times* reported that the Germans must somehow have overwhelmed the great forts of Liège, and were now in Brussels. The war was not yet three weeks old, and the Germans were occupying the capital city of one of their opponents! Four days later readers were told of THE BRITISH ARMY'S STERN FIGHT.

British and Germans had met at a place called Mons, and the retreat from Mons had begun. On the last day in August *The Times* headlines proclaimed THE FIERCEST FIGHT IN HISTORY. Heavy losses of British troops was admitted. But the broken British regiments, heads bloody but unbowed, their honour still untarnished, gallantly battled on against great odds. This news, far from disheartening the British public, sent a record 30,000 to the recruiting stations on 1st September. On 4th September came a news item about the progress of the "Russian steamroller". Our eastern allies had won a great victory at Lemburg. The news of the disastrous Russian defeat at Tannenburg, which had taken place the week before, did not reach the British public until later. On 6th September, with the war scarcely a month old, the German threat to Paris was admitted. Two days later came the welcome news that the German advance had at last been checked, and on 9th September readers were greeted by the jubilant headline, THE TURN OF THE TIDE.

The exhausted Germans were in full retreat, with the British and the French in hot pursuit. At this rate of progress the Germans would soon be back where they belonged, and to where they had started with such grandiose hopes six weeks before. Hopes that the war would be over by Christmas, almost dead a week before, now revived. Then came the news that the Germans did not give in so easily. They had entrenched themselves on the northern slopes of the River Aisne, and had actually checked the Allied advance. Trench warfare had begun. The Germans had lost the Battle of the Marne, but they did not feel that they had yet lost the war. So the journalists, as far as the censor would allow them, brought home to the British public the realities of the new situation.

One of the most popular authors of the day was Mr. H. G. Wells. In the first few hectic weeks of the war he produced a short, forceful book entitled *The War that will end War*, which enjoyed a wide circulation. In simple language he explained that it would not be sufficient to put the Germans back over the Belgian border, and to tell them not to do it again. It was a matter of, either destroy this great German Empire, or be destroyed by it. We must therefore brace ourselves to carry on fighting until these Germans really knew that they were beaten, and protested that they had had enough of war. But there must be no hatred of the German people. We must confine our hatred to the evil system inspired by the mental and moral corruption that had taken possession of the German imagination and way of life. We must learn the lesson of 1871, when the Germans defeated the French, but failed to smash French imperialism. We must avoid a vindictive triumph. We were fighting for the British way of life against Prussian militarism, to defend and extend the possibilities of civilisation. Young men should, therefore, enlist for the sake of changing the world.

"There must be no hatred of the German people," declared Mr. Wells, optimistically. War had scarcely begun when hatred for people with German names or connections speedily made itself felt. Butchers, bakers, barbers and anyone with a German name found it expedient to anglicise it, sometimes after their shops had been wrecked and looted. No rumour about "the enemy in our midst" was too stupid not to be believed. Bakers were mixing slow poison in the bread and cakes. Others were spies. They were signalling to German submarines off the coast. Some were planning to overpower railway signalmen, and to wreck trains. That prosperous businessman whose family came over from Germany years ago, constructed that hard tennis court with a view to turning it into a gun platform when the time comes. In fact all the German master spies in Britain were rounded up within a few hours of the outbreak of war. Enemy aliens were likewise rounded up, and interned in a special camp in the Isle of Man.

Some music lovers now declared their utter abhorrence of all music of German origin. Sir Henry Wood received numerous letters exhorting him to exclude all music by German composers from his promenade concerts at the Queen's Hall. In deference to public opinion he suspended concerts of Wagner's music, for a while. When feeling had died down somewhat he re-instated them.

Twenty-two-year-old Cecil Roberts, the future author of *Victoria 4-30,* and other novels, was holidaying at Skegness when

29

war broke out. Entertaining his fellow boarders with a rendering of Beethoven's *Moonlight Sonata* on the piano, he was rudely interrupted by an aggressive lady. "How *dare* you play that filthy German music?" she demanded to know. "It's an outrage! Why don't you go home and enlist?" A plain spoken little man from the north country answered her: "Nay! I'll tell thee summat! Why should a bonny lad go and sacrifice himself for a withered old geezer like you?" To which pertinent question the aggressive lady had no effective reply!

Music for the troops was another topical issue. The new armies deserved new marching songs, topical words set to well known tunes. To the lively tune of *John Peel* it was suggested that the lads marched to war singing:

> D'ye ken John French with his khaki suit,
> His belt and his gaiters and his stout brown boot,
> Along with his guns, his horse and his foot,
> On the road to Berlin in the morning.

To the tune of *Here's to the maiden* topical words like these were fitted:

> Here's to Lord Kitchener, brown with the sun,
> Here's to John Jellicoe, first in command . . . etc.

Similar soul stirring words were fitted to other well known melodies. But, sad to say, this well meant endeavour to provide the new armies with new marching songs found no favour with the men they were intended to inspire and enhearten. The soldiers of 1914, on their route marches along the roads and lanes of old England, proved decidedly shy about publicly extolling the virtues and excellencies of French, Kitchener, Jellicoe and other national heroes. When they lifted up their voices in song it was to ask personal questions like: "Who's your lady friend?" and in other music hall hits of the day. To well known tunes they later found words of their own that expressed their true feelings. To the tune of *Here's to the maiden* they preferred to sing:

> Why did I join the army, boys?
> I must have been . . . well barmy.

At church parade services they sometimes sang the hymn, *What a Friend we have in Jesus.* On secular occasions they made use of the tune to other words which expressed their deepest longing:

> When this . . . war is over,
> No more soldiering for me.

Among those who found the business of adjusting to the new situation especially difficult were some of the left wing politicians. Ramsay MacDonald resigned the leadership of the Labour Party, in favour of Arthur Henderson. The official policy of the Labour Party, to which they adhered throughout the war, was "We condemn the policy which has produced the war. We do not obstruct the war effort, but our duty is to secure peace at the earliest possible moment." Ramsay MacDonald refused to give his support to recruiting campaigns. Within a nation at war he felt called to co-operate with those who aimed to preserve a regard for peace. This, he felt was vital if the soldiers were not to be betrayed by a vindictive peace settlement. He bade the Trade Unions do their duty, and at the same time to be thinking of the eventual settlement with Germany at the end of the war. He saw the danger of the militarising of the British mind. If that happened, whatever came to pass on the battlefronts, Germany had won the war. She would have Prussianised Britain! For standing by these principles he was denounced at various times as a pacifist, a pro-German and a traitor.

James Keir Hardie, a pacifist and the founder of the Labour Party, had even graver problems. His faith in the international solidarity of the working classes was rudely shattered when the workers of the world signally failed to unite in the cause of peace. In the first weeks of the war, addressing his constituents at Merthyr, he was shouted down by a howling mob, who followed him to the home of a friend. A very unkind, and unjust, cartoon portrayed him accepting a bag of money from the Kaiser. Under the cartoon were the words:

> Also the Nobel prize (though tardy),
> I now confer on Keir von Hardie.

He was the first Labour Member of Parliament, the only Member to stand by pacifist principles, and he died of a broken heart on 29th September, 1915.

The suffragettes, those ladies who had been so violent as well as vocal, in their demands for the vote, found the matter of adjustment comparatively easy. The National Union of Women's Suffrage Societies, and the Women's Social and Political Union, called a truce, and placed themselves unreservedly behind the war effort. With shrewd commonsense Mrs. Pankhurst asked: "What would be the good of a vote without a country to vote in?" The Government responded by setting free the hundreds of suffragettes from their prisons.

One who agreed with Mrs. Pankhurst's point of view was Robert Blatchford, the author, journalist and founder of the Socialist weekly, *The Clarion*. For years Blatchford had seen the inevitability of war, and tried to warn his compatriots of the German menace, but with little success. Blatchford, a soldier in his younger days, felt that defeat by Germany meant also the defeat of all those social purposes he had spent his life to achieve. The only way out of the impasse, he declared, was an Allied victory. Many of his fellow Socialists profoundly disagreed with him. The circulation of *The Clarion* dropped from 60,000 to 10,000, and it ceased publication. In August and September, 1914, Blatchford watched the young men and girls on the seaside promenades, walking arm in arm, laughing, listening to the band, oblivious of what lay in store for so many of them. He found something profoundly disturbing in the cheerfulness, the unawareness of impending danger, and the total absence of bitterness and anger. One sunny day in September he stood among a jubilant crowd watching the 2nd Bn. Scots Guards marching to Waterloo Station, to entrain for the seats of war. The band played *Tipperary,* and the crowd broke into singing. The scene was one of joyous excitement, with no hint of any awareness of the dire peril into which the smiling, singing soldiers were going. Four short weeks later, after being involved in desperate fighting in the trenches near Ypres, those same 2nd Bn. Scots Guards were moved back into reserve, their numbers reduced to 450.

As advocates of the Gospel of Peace the Churches were in a difficult position. The Society of Friends (Quakers) issued their special declaration.

"Christ demands of us that we adhere, without swerving, to the methods of love. Therefore, if any seeming conflict should arise between His service and that of the State, it is to Christ that our supreme loyalty should be given, whatever be the consequences."[2]

"The methods of love"[3]—but suppose adopting the methods of love towards the Germans resulted in their occupation of Britain, and that Prussianising of our country of which Ramsay MacDonald and others were afraid? Would we have our children grow up in a Prussianised Britain? We ought to love the wicked Germans, but we ought to love our wives and children even more. The Churches generally resolved their dilemma by ranging themselves behind the war effort.

"Our conscience is clear as to the justice and necessity of the war. It simply could not be avoided, and we feel confident that by God's help it will be brought to a successful issue . . .

33

shall not our single men be the first to offer themselves?"

Thus a typical passage in the parish magazines in September 1914. The Bishop of London, the Right Reverend A. F. Winnington-Ingram, graphically described the conflict as between the Nailed Hand and the Iron Fist. Parsons gave talks and lectures on topics like, "Then and now—the Two Attilas", comparing the 5th century King of the Huns with the 20th century one.

The year 1914 ended with the British people beginning to adjust themselves to the new demands of life in wartime. Across the Channel the war of movement had ended, and a trench system ran from the North Sea to the Swiss frontier. Like it or not, the British people were beginning to realise that they were called upon to prepare themselves for yet unknown and far-reaching changes involved in a long war of attrition. Business as usual? What a hope!

Chapter 4

A TASTE OF REAL WAR

"IT would do the British public good to have a taste of what the army is up against!" exclaimed an un-named and exasperated soldier in the early months of the war. As the weeks and months went by the gap of sympathy and understanding between the soldier at the Front and the civilian at home steadily widened. The soldier in the trenches, suffering the physical discomforts of cold, and vermin, plus the constant threat of violent and sudden death, felt increasingly out of touch with those at home, for whom life still went on safely and comfortably. The war was in its fifth month when the German navy gave the British public its first taste of real war, in the shape of a brisk and destructive bombardment. Early in the morning of 16th December, 1914, as the good people of Hartlepool, Scarborough and Whitby rose from their beds, ate their breakfasts and prepared for the day's work, a German battle cruiser squadron appeared off the coast to shatter their calm. Osbert Sitwell later convincingly described the scene that morning in his novel *Before the Bombardment*.

Hartlepool suffered worst, although the Territorials stationed there brought three 6 in. guns into action against the raiders. The Germans fired 1,500 shells into the town. 500 houses, the railway station, the waterworks, a gasometer and the battery were hit. 113 civilians and 7 soldiers were killed. 300 civilians and 14 soldiers suffered wounds. Scarborough and Whitby, both undefended towns, escaped more lightly. When the bombardment of "the Queen of the Watering Places" began, many people fled to the railway station, and boarded the train then about to leave for Hull. Nevertheless, 18 people were killed and 100 were wounded. At Whitby, "as is inevitable in German warfare," the *Daily Mirror* caustically observed, shellfire damaged the Abbey.

The British public had had their first real taste of war, and quite naturally, they hated it. The threefold bombardment came as a tremendous shock to a people who regarded their shores as safe, behind the sure shield of the British navy. How did it come to pass that German warships could, with impunity, approach within three miles of our coasts, kill hundreds of defenceless citizens, and then escape in the mists of the North Sea? The gentlemen at the Admiralty tried to explain that demonstrations of this kind were devoid of military significance. Admittedly they caused loss of civilian life and property, and this was much to be regretted. Public anger was great, and the official explanations did little to allay it.

After the shells came the bombs. Ignoring the close proximity of the season of peace and goodwill, a German aeroplane dropped the first bomb on England at Dover, on Christmas Eve, 1914. The only casualty was a cabbage in a field. On Christmas Day a German plane was observed flying over Sheerness, but no bombs were dropped. After these two harmless demonstrations came the dreaded Zeppelins, those monster airships named after their inventor, Count Ferdinand von Zeppelin, a man very highly thought of by the Kaiser. January, 1915, brought the first British deaths as a result of enemy action in the air. On the night of 19-20th January two Zeppelins appeared over Norfolk. Two people were killed at Great Yarmouth and two at King's Lynn. On the night of 22nd-23rd February a German plane dropped bombs, mainly in fields, near Colchester, Braintree and Coggeshall. They smashed the backs of some houses, but no casualties were reported.

The Zeppelins were back in April, this time over Tyneside,

Plate 1—Scene at Buckingham Palace on the outbreak of war, 1914.
(Photo: Imperial War Museum.)

Plate 2—Londoners in the Strand reading the first bulletin from the front, 1914.
(*Photo: Hulton Picture Library.*)

dropping bombs at intervals near Blyth and Wallsend. All the lights on the north east coast were extinguished, with the exception of searchlights which came into immediate operation. No one was killed or injured, though some damage was done to property.

So far London had escaped attack. Not until the night of 31st May-1st June did a Zeppelin venture over the metropolis. This was the first of 25 air raids by Zeppelins and aeroplanes between 1915 and 1918. On 8th September, 1915, a bus was blown to pieces outside Liverpool Street Station, only two passengers escaping alive. £500,000 worth of damage to property was also caused on that occasion. The most destructive raid on the capital city was a daylight one on 13th June, 1917. On that lovely summer morning 22 planes dropped nearly 100 bombs killing 162 people, injuring 432, besides destroying much property. The killed included 18 children in their school at Poplar. On 24th September that same year planes rained down bombs on Finsbury, Islington, King's Cross, Soho, Holborn and Piccadilly. Outside the Bedford Hotel, in Southampton Row, a bronze tablet later recorded that "On and around these steps twelve persons were killed, and many injured, by a bomb dropped from a German aeroplane."

Another ghastly tragedy occurred on the night of 28th January, 1918, when a 112 lb. incendiary bomb crashed through the roof of Odham's building, in Long Acre. It tore its way down into the basement killing 35 people who had taken shelter there, and injuring nearly 100. Moonless or foggy nights rendered the raiders harmless. Weather conditions brought about the complete failure of a raid by 11 Zeppelins on London and the Midlands, in October, 1916.

During the whole of the year 1915 the raiders met with no serious opposition. In the early months of 1916 observer posts were set up, complete with warning devices to amplify the sound of the approaching enemy aircraft, enabling their direction to be judged. The year 1916 also produced the invention which proved fatal to the huge Zeppelins—the incendiary bullet, fired from the new fighter planes. Considerable progress was also made in the efficiency of the anti-aircraft gun. The "box barrage", a cone of fire from the anti-aircraft guns, placed round the attacker, was one device to harass the raiders.

On 4th September, 1916, the morning papers came out with exultant headlines like, BLAZING ZEPPELIN FALLS NEAR LONDON. Readers were informed of the total failure of the most ambitious air raid yet carried out by the enemy. Thirteen Zeppelins, intent upon striking a blow at the heart of the British Empire, approached London and the industrial Midlands. Three approached London, and two of them were driven ignominiously off. The third of these products of the misguided ingenuity of Count Zeppelin, 780 ft. in length, made aerial history. Approaching Enfield, she was picked up by searchlights, and attacked by both anti-aircraft guns and fighter planes. The thousands of spectators saw the airship burst into a great mass of flames, and crash into a field at Cuffley. Everybody cheered, railway engine drivers hooted madly on their whistles, in many places the National Anthem was sung, and there was a rush from miles around to view the remains of the burned out airship. The other twelve Zeppelins, defeated by the new lighting restrictions, dropped their bombs promiscuously over East Anglia, and ran for home. The results—two civilians killed and thirteen injured, and no military damage of any kind sustained, though some non-military property suffered damage. But the enemy lost, not only the expensive Zeppelin, but also her entire crew, numbering probably 36. Less than a month later, on 1st October, another Zeppelin suffered a spectacular demise, this time at Potter's Bar, in Middlesex. Lieut. W. J. Tempest attacked the giant in his fighter plane, and brought her down in flames by well aimed incendiary bullets. From this time onwards Zeppelin attacks died down, to be superceded by a new terror, the Gotha biplane, purpose built for bombing, fitted with twin engines, and with a speed of 70-80 m.p.h. Reference has already been made to some of the damage they did. Count von Zeppelin, who died on 8th March, 1917, lived just long enough to see the failure of his monsters as an effective instrument of war. The defences against air attack steadily improved, and, in 1917, 21 Gothas were shot down, either by fighter planes or by fire from anti-aircraft guns. The Gothas made their last raid on London on the night of 19th-20th May, 1918. Between 30 and 40 planes took part, and they killed 49 people, and injured 177. This was the last air raid of proportions of the First World War. The total British air raid casualties of the First World numbered 1,413 killed, and 3,407 injured. The London area's share of this slaughter was 587 killed and 1,627 injured. The comparative figures for the Second World War were 60,585 killed and 86,175 wounded in Great Britain, including the 29,980 killed and 50,497 injured in the London area.

Hartlepool, Scarborough and Whitby were not the only towns to receive the attentions of the German navy. Great Yarmouth and Lowestoft were bombarded by German battle cruisers on 25th April, 1916. Lowestoft was bombarded again, in November that same year. Great Yarmouth, which had suffered her first raid on 3rd November, 1914, was visited again on 14th January, 1918. A German torpedo boat fired 50 shells into the town, killing four people.

The Yorkshire seaport of Hull was never bombarded by the German navy, but air raids were frequent. The Rev. C. H. Hulbert, a Wesleyan minister stationed in Hull from 1914 to 1921, described how, when the alarm was given, unnumbered people would flock to the open country, with as many of their belongings as they could carry on their carts and prams. Mr. Hulbert was minister at the Thornton Hall, a building seating 2,000 people, filled with worshippers every Sunday evening. The roof lights were blacked out, the windows curtained, and in the event of an air raid warning, the people were invited to go quietly home.

In comparison with the Second World War the British public

escaped lightly in the matter of air raid and naval casualties. The total number of killed and wounded in the First World War raids on Britain was less than 5,000. How did they react to this taste of real war? According to historian A. J. P. Taylor those few shells and bombs caused more hysteria in England than the military massacres on the Western Front.

Chapter 5

ANTI-GERMAN

WILD BEASTS FIGHTING UNDER THE GERMAN FLAG proclaimed the front page of the *Daily Sketch* on 9th January, 1915. Under the headline appeared pictures of eight hard-faced German generals. Page 2 of the same edition gave extracts from the French Commission of Enquiry into German atrocities in Belgium. In the Province of Namur alone it was alleged that the Germans had "shot like rats," 3,000 of the 300,000 inhabitants of the province. A woman of 98 bayoneted in her bed, a boy of 14 disembowelled, a harmless old man of 78 shot in the street, and in the town of Dinant alone 31 children under the age of 15 were shot, were among the long list of accusations. The main culprits, according to the report, were the Bavarians. In addition to this murder of civilians it was alleged that innumerable women and girls were the victims of the brutal lust of the German soldiery. In view of this young male readers were asked CAN YOU STILL HANG BACK? IT MAY BE YOUR SISTER NEXT. The Report bluntly declared that incendiarism, pillage and murder were as much a part of the German military equipment as their big guns.

We have already noted the appearance of anti-German feeling in the very early stages of the war. One of its manifestations was a suspicion of any one with a German sounding name. One of the earliest victims of this suspicion was the First Sea Lord, Prince Louis of Battenberg, son of Prince Alexander of Hesse.

Prince Louis had been a naturalised British subject since the age of 14. In the Austrian war of 1866 Prince Louis' father had fought against Prussia. But when the dreadnought *Audacious* was sunk by a mine off the Irish coast, a whispering campaign began against the First Sea Lord. This crusade against enemies in high places was ably led by Mr. Horatio Bottomley, through his widely read and influential weekly *John Bull.* As a result of this vulgar outcry against his German origin Prince Louis resigned from office on 29th November, 1914, and Lord Fisher was appointed in his place.

The German naval raids of December, 1914, added intensity to the anti-German feeling. The year 1915 saw a steady growth of hatred. Mounting British casualties at Neuve Chapelle, Ypres, Gallipoli and Loos, the sinking of the *Lusitania,* Zeppelin raids and the execution of Nurse Cavell all combined to increase anti-German feeling among the British people.

May, 1915, brought the resignation of the Lord Chancellor, Lord Haldane. As Secretary of State for War from 1905 until 1912, he founded the Territorial Army, and created an Imperial General Staff. A distinguished student of philosophy, someone remembered that he had once said that Germany was his spiritual home. Lord Haldane meant the Germany of men like Goethe and Schiller, not of the Hohenzollerns. Rumour said that he was an illegitimate brother of the Kaiser, and in secret communication with the German government. The very worst conclusions were drawn about the purpose of his official visit to Germany in 1912. Although he was a lifelong bachelor, of blameless life, rumour credited him with a German wife. A press campaign against him resulted in his resignation in May, 1915.

The sinking of the *Lusitania,* with a loss of 1,198 lives, including 114 Americans, was the occasion for anti-German riots in the East End of London. Anyone whose name might be considered German was in danger. The mob raided a baker's shop in Poplar, and began to throw sacks of flour from an upper window. One of these fell squarely on the helmet of a policeman, who was vainly trying to control the crowd, covering him with flour from head to foot. Smithfield Meat Market was the scene of more ugly scenes when porters mobbed butchers of German origin, and roughly hustled them out of the market. There were wild scenes at the usually sedate Stock Exchange, when City men passed a resolution that: "all Germans, whether naturalised or not, must go." Barbers and butchers, as well as bakers, were victims of the rioting. In some cases their shops were looted and their furniture thrown out into the street.

Anti-German rioting also broke out in Liverpool, Manchester and Birkenhead. No less than 200 shops were attacked in Liverpool alone, doing an estimated £40,000 worth of damage. The police managed to arrest some of the ringleaders of the riots. Thames Police Court magistrates inflicted fines upon them ranging from 1/6d to 20/-, with the alternative of imprisonment. One man, alleged to have led an attack on a German shop shouting: "Come on boys they're Germans; let's have them out of it!," was fined 10/-, with the alternative of six days in prison. The magistrate told him that he ought to be drilling. The sinking of the *Lusitania,* following hard upon the 2nd Battle of Ypres and the Dardenelles landing, produced a further hardening of feelings against the Germans.

Lord Derby, in a letter to the press, described the use of poisonous gases by the Germans at Ypres, and the *Lusitania* sinking as "two diabolical acts of brutal and premeditated murder." England therefore no longer called for men to fight an honourable foe, but for men to join to hunt down and crush once and for all, a race of cold-blooded murderers. He called for more recruits, promising them that they would be present when the day of reckoning came, and bitter vengeance was taken. He called upon the men of Britain to prepare themselves for the day of revenge. The *Daily Mail* published a photograph of the corpses of four infant victims of the *Lusitania* disaster, "in the hope of making everyone in this country realise how war in the twentieth century has been degraded by the barbarity of the

German government and people."[1]

The intensified feeling against Germany showed itself in countless ways—a patriotic lady pasting a strip over the name "Bechstein" on her piano; the Bechstein Hall in London, changing its name to the Wigmore Hall; a mindless mob kicking to death a dachshund in a London street. Gustav Theodore von Holst, the composer of the *Planets Suite*, of Swedish descent, born in Cheltenham in 1874, found it expedient to drop the "von" from his name. The Battenburgs altered their family name to Mountbatten, and the Royal Family from Guelph to Windsor. Captain Weiner, an American millionaire of Austrian extraction, fell under grave suspicion on account of a heavy concrete platform he had laid for a lake in his garden at Ewell Castle, and in connection with the observatory tower, complete with telescope, in the same garden. The platform could have been used as an emplacement for a heavy gun directed against London. He explained the purpose of the platform, and also that the tower and telescope were designed for sporting, rather than military purposes. When, in October, 1915, a Zeppelin flew over London, an Englishman called Usher, and a hotel manager, a Swiss, climbed on to the roof of the hotel. Rather incautiously Usher lit a cigarette. This was seen from below, and Mr. Usher was brought to Court, charged with signalling to the enemy. Commonsense prevailed, and the case was dismissed amid laughter in Court.

Not so fortunate was Sir Edgar Speyer, a German born banker, and a British subject since 1892. He was a great friend of British music, and was associated with Sir Henry Wood for many years. In 1902 Sir Edgar founded the Queen's Hall Orchestra Ltd., to ensure the future of that band of musicians. He was also one of the founders of the Whitechapel Art Gallery, and a generous donor to various charities. He was created a baronet in 1906, and a Privy Counsellor three years later. When war came Speyer tried to resign at Privy Counsellor, and to revoke his baronetcy, but King George refused to allow this. Public opinion caused him

Plate 3—H.E. The French Ambassador in London inspecting the wreckage of the German naval airship L33 shot down near Little Wigborough on 23rd September 1916. (*Photo: Imperial War Museum.*)

Plate 4—Zeppelin wrecked in 1916 showing remains of engine.
(Photo: Hulton Picture Library.)

to retire to the U.S.A. in 1915.

Two other eminent businessmen, Sir John Brunner and Sir Alfred Mond, successfully sued an over-enthusiastic patriot who rashly described them as German swine. A man who said that he had heard a British officer say that he had seen an alleged hospital ship at Alexandria disgorge, not wounded, but 2,000 British soldiers, was fined £100, and sent to prison for a month, to teach him the folly of "spreading by mouth a false report." *John Bull* fiercely attacked the Rev. Hewlett Johnson, Vicar of St. Margaret's, Altrincham, who was chaplain to the German prisoner-of-war camp in that parish, for placing flowers on the grave of a German prisoner who had died in the camp.

Sir Arthur Conan-Doyle, creator of Sherlock Holmes, wrote an angry letter to *The Times* in December, 1917, denouncing German outrages upon British prisoners of war. He called for "implacable hatred against the perpetrators." When he was reproved by the Dean of Manchester for excessive anti-German feeling, he defended himself with the plea of "righteous indignation."

In the summer of 1918 widespread interest was aroused by a report of a Black Book compiled by German secret agents. This remarkable volume was alleged to contain the records of the moral weaknesses and sexual vices of no less than 47,000 Englishmen and women. The 47,000 included members of the Royal Household, Privy Counsellors, Cabinet Ministers, and their wives, judges, bankers, editors and others. The joke question of the hour became: "Is *your* name in the Black Book?" The purpose of this catalogue of eminent names was to extract information from them, under the threat of exposure. The immediate occasion of this revelation was the trial of Mr. Pemberton Billing, the Independent Member for East Herts. He was sued for libel by a dancer whom he accused of sexual perversion for a dance she performed at a private performance of Oscar Wilde's banned play, *The Vision of Salome*. The trial lasted six days, Mr. Pemberton Billing citing the Black Book in his defence to such good effect that he was acquitted.

This last summer of the war also witnessed a resurgence of feeling against what enemy aliens were still at large. The biggest crowd since the outbreak of the war gathered in Trafalgar Square on 14th July, demanding the immediate internment of all enemy aliens. Since the springtime the war had seemed to be going again in favour of the Germans. They had pushed back the Allied forces, and once again Paris seemed to be in danger. The rumble of the enemy guns was so great as to be heard in south east England. Against this background of anxiety the feeling against all enemy aliens was expressed in the slogan: "Intern them all." Similar meetings were held in other parts of the country, a notable one being in the Free Trade Hall, Manchester. So intense was the feeling aroused that a petition, two miles long, and containing 1,250,000 signatures, was rolled up like a drum and delivered to the Prime Minister at his residence in Downing Street. The signatories demanded the immediate internment of all enemy aliens without distinction. This sweeping request involved German born men who had married English wives, and had a son, or sons, fighting for England. The authorities complied with public demand by rounding up a further 300 aliens by the end of August.

Amid the general hysterical outcries against the wicked Germans there were those who tried to separate fact from fiction, and to act accordingly. Cecil Roberts and his mother walked out of church during the course of the vicar's fiery diatribe against the unspeakable Huns. Our foes had cut off the hands of Belgian children, and crucified a Canadian soldier. Our gallant British lads were the warriors of the Lord, and upon them depended the survival of Christian civilisation. In contrast to this the Society of Friends founded an Emergency Fund for the assistance of enemy aliens—Germans, Austrians and Hungarians—in distress. They also helped the British born wives of interned aliens on a relief scale of 10/- per week, and 1/6d for each child. The small army of women volunteers who carried out this work, visited,

46

reported upon and assessed deserving cases. After the *Lusitania* riots 75 aliens, whose homes were wrecked, were sheltered and fed in the Friends' Meeting House in north London for more than a month.

The British people on this side of the North Sea hated the Germans much more than the British people—the armed forces —on the other side of the North Sea, who were in actual contact with them. To many of those safely at home the Germans were "wild beasts", and "Huns". The soldier's term was more usually : "Jerry", a comrade in distress. The civilian at home neither saw nor knew the realities of trench warfare. The soldier not only saw and knew, but to him fell the awesome task of killing and maiming men who were as civilised as he was. The soldier on leave noticed that the really big catastrophes like the Dardenelles, and the Somme, were too great for the general public to grasp. Their limit was the small disasters that struck their own land, like the naval bombardment of Scarborough and the occasional air raids. Anti-German propaganda in Britain, aimed at transforming the enemy into wild beasts and devils, and at presenting the war as a conflict between light and darkness, heaven against hell, had substantial success with millions of respectable citizens.

Chapter 6

ANTI-WAR

THE anti-war movement in Britain was confined to a small minority of mainly educated people. But though small in numbers the anti-war brigade impressed authority as potentially dangerous, and was accordingly under constant suspicion and surveillance, and sometimes suffered grievous persecution. Anti-war feeling grew as the years of slaughter rolled on, taxing severely the seemingly endless patience of the ordinary man and woman. A marked growth in anti-war feeling was noted after the rejection of the German peace overtures in 1916, and after the Russian Revolution in 1917.

The coming of conscription brought the movement into the open. In the closing months of 1914 recruits poured in quicker than they could be handled. 900,000 had volunteered by the end of 1914, and still they surged forward at the rate of 30,000 per week. Many of these volunteers would have been more use to the war effort if they had stayed in their workshops. Many of them were fathers, anxious to "do their bit", in spite of the many single men still at home. A householders' return, in November, 1914, secured a return of men who were willing to serve in the armed forces, but who were then not eligible. A circular letter bearing the signatures of Asquith, Bonar Law and Henderson, appealed to every eligible man to hold himself in readiness to enlist. In those early days much Liberal and Socialist opinion was against conscription on principle. 1915 brought the "Derby scheme", associated with Lord Derby, director-general of recruiting. After the National Registration Act had produced a complete Register of the population, men were invited to "attest" their willingness for potential army service, even though they were now needed at home. They would be called up in groups, starting with the youngest, and the unmarried. This was the last effort to retain the voluntary system, and it failed to produce the number of recruits required to fill the gaps torn in the ranks by the exigencies of cruel war. Accordingly the first Compulsory Service Act was passed in January, 1916.

The coming of conscription had been anticipated by the anti-war section of the community since August, 1914. The No Conscription Fellowship was already in being, organised and prepared for action when the expected compulsory military service was officially decreed. In 1915 there was a large response to a letter in the *Labour Leader,* organ of the Independent Labour Party, inviting all who intended to refuse military service to enroll, and to meet together to work out an effective policy. Clifford Allen was appointed chairman of the Fellowship, and when he went to prison for his principles, Bertrand Russell took his place. Fenner Brockway was appointed secretary. Throughout the war the Fellowship bore the brunt of the opposition occasioned by their anti-war stand. The avowed aim of the Fellowship was: "the unfettered right of every man to decide for himself the issues of life and death."

Dr. Maude Royden, a gentle but passionate woman, a partial cripple from birth, who was Assistant Preacher at the London City Temple from 1917-20, founded the Fellowship of Reconciliation in 1915. Dr. Royden pointed out that though war was undoubtedly evil, it was also a great adventure for the millions who had volunteered. Their motives were partly patriotic, and partly a desire to escape from the drabness and dreariness which passed for life for so many in those early twentieth century days.

The coming of conscription also provoked the establishment of the National Council for Civil Liberties. This was an all-party movement, chiefly Labour, and with the addition

49   4

of Dr. John Clifford, the Free Church leader, and the Bishop of Hereford. Their aims were to maintain the right of free speech, to resist industrial conscription, and to reform, and if possible repeal, the Military Service Act. The coming into being of the Council was inspired by the violent breaking up of public meetings, and by police raids on the offices of the *Labour Leader*. The need for such an organisation was apparent when their own public meeting, in the Memorial Hall, Farringdon Street, was broken up, and the speakers were not even allowed to reach the platform.

The Friends' Service Committee also predictably pronounced themselves against conscription. They announced : "We regard the central conception of the Military Service Act as imperilling the liberty of the individual conscience, which is the main hope of human progress, and of entrenching more deeply that Militarism from which we all desire the world to be freed."

Sylvia Pankhurst was another objector. In the summer of 1916 she organised a procession to Trafalgar Square for the purpose of holding an anti-conscription rally. "An open act of sedition," declared the press, and invited true patriots to break up the meeting. Some true patriots accepted the invitation, and drove the speakers from the plinth of Nelson's Column by means of a bombardment of packets of red and yellow ochre.

Soon after the Act came into force the War Office and the Salvation Army entered into a warm argument. The Act exempted ministers of religion from conscription. But were the full-time officers of the Salvation Army ministers of religion within the meaning of the Act? They had not been ordained, either by a bishop or any other dignitary. The Salvationists, under their General, Bramwell Booth, stood firm, and the gentlemen at Whitehall were compelled to admit the validity of the claim that Salvation Army officers were genuine ministers of religion.

From March, 1916, all single men were liable to be conscripted, and from May of that year, all married men, in each case between the ages of 18 and 41. As the massacres on the Western Front continued, a further Act, in March, 1918, raised the calling up age to 51. The Labour movement in general agreed that conscription was necessary. Employers were asked to co-operate by certifying which men could be spared, and which men were essential to maintain production. Some employers eagerly grasped this opportunity to rid themselves of agitators and other troublemakers.

In towns all over the country Tribunals were set up before which those who claimed exemption from military service must appear. Three grounds for exemption were specified—conscience, indispensability and hardship. These Tribunals consisted of local worthies like town councillors, magistrates, industrialists and a representative of the military authorities. Women, as well as men, were eligible to serve on the Tribunals. Those who claimed exemption on grounds of indispensability or hardship generally had a much smoother passage than those who objected on grounds of conscience. They discovered that Prime Minister Lloyd George's threat: "I shall consider the best means of making the path of that class (i.e. the conscientious objectors) a hard one," had substance. In some places it appeared that one qualification for membership of a Tribunal was a zeal for recruiting for the Armed Forces. The Tribunal was supposed to judge the sincerity of the applicant. The Act itself was not particularly helpful, in that it did not define the word "conscientious." Each Tribunal was left to find its own interpretation. The Tribunals could exempt an objector from all military and other service, or direct him to work of national importance, or into a non-combatant unit where he would dig trenches, erect barbed wired entanglements or become a stretcher bearer. But first the objector must satisfy the Tribunal of his sincerity. That was no easy task, even for the more intellectual objectors. Those who objected to war on the grounds that it was contrary to the spirit and teaching of Christ could expect as rough a passage as those who objected to having to

51

fight for Capitalism. One Christian man was asked :

"Do you believe that war is sinful?"

"Yes."

"Do you believe that the blood of Christ cleanses from all sin?"

"Yes."

"Then you would be forgiven if you took part in wars."

In all 16,000 men refused to fight, whether or not the Tribunals recognised their sincerity. Three quarters of them were Socialists, refusing to fight for Capitalism. The rest objected mainly on religious grounds. The smaller denominations were prominent here, rather than the larger ones. Christadelphians, Pentecostalists, 7th Day Adventists, Plymouth Brethren and Jehovah's Witnesses were all represented. In their preaching they called attention to the imminence of the 2nd Coming of Christ, after the forces of evil had been defeated at Armageddon, the district of Megiddo, in Palestine. In the later stages of the war General Allenby and his cavalry actually chased the Turks over this region.

Among the larger denominations the Methodists provided 140 conscientious objectors. The Wesleyan Methodist Peace Fellowship, founded in 1916, numbered 90 ministerial and 1,000 lay members by the end of the war. The Society of Friends proved not to be the solidly Pacifist body they were reputed to be. Only 45.4 per cent of their men of military age declared themselves conscientious objectors, and 33.6 per cent enlisted. The Quaker pacifism was traditional, rather than doctrinal—in a body that set loose specific doctrinal standards.

16,000 men refused to fight, and were ready to take the consequences. Failing to make a case before the Tribunals they were drafted into the army. If they failed to report for duty they were deemed deserters. This meant being court martialled and threatened with death. In May, 1916, 34 conscientious objectors were sent to France, and told that they would be shot as deserters if they persisted in their refusal to fight. Prime

Minister Asquith intervened, and their sentences were commuted to ten years penal servitude. In all 1,500 objectors braved the courts martial, and served sentences in civil gaols. Here they were often harshly treated. At Dartmoor six objectors, all professional men, were put to work on the antiquated treadmill, turning out six sacks of oats per day. Ten men would be harnessed to a cart for the transportation of coke. Others were set digging a field, although a horse and plough were available.

34 objectors heard themselves sentenced to death—although the sentence was never carried out.

31 objectors were driven mad by the inhuman treatment meted out to them.

73 objectors died as a direct result of their sentences involving many months of exhausting hard labour on an inadequate diet.

When the Armistice was signed the authorities were in no hurry to release the objectors from prison. The year 1919 was well advanced before all of them were set free.

In the House of Commons Ramsay MacDonald and Philip Snowden championed the objectors' cause. The last-named wrote a scathing pamphlet under the title, "British Prussianism : The Scandal of the Tribunals". Another critic pointed out how polite the Tribunals could be to publicans claiming exemption to military service on the grounds of the importance of their calling. Yet another sharp critic of the Tribunals was Dr. John Clifford : "I am ashamed of my country," he wrote. "The Tribunals are a disgrace to our name. I know what it is to oppose a war (he had opposed the Boer War), and I know what it is to defend a war." For many years past Dr. Clifford had been swift to come to the aid of people penalised for the sake of their principles. It would take more than even the hysteria generated by the First World War to divert him from *his* principles!

At the end of 1917 the government, noting the growth of the anti-war spirit, put into operation Clause 27C of the Defence of the Realm Act (DORA). All writings about the war, and the making of peace, were to be submitted to the Censor before publication. The Society of Friends decided to disobey, and published a pamphlet entitled *A Challenge to Militarism*. This pamphlet exposed some of the truth about the treatment of conscientious objectors in gaol. As a result the acting secretary of the Friends' Service Committee, Edith Ellis, was fined £100, and ordered to pay 50 guineas costs, or else go to prison for three months. An appeal was dismissed. The judge, in dismissing the appeal, expressed his horror that "educated people have given utterance to sentiments of the utmost disloyalty." No doubt he would have agreed fully with the Anglican prison chaplain who told his conscientious objector prisoners that they ought to be drowned!

Because of his support for the No Conscription Fellowship, and his scathing views about the stupidity of war as a means of settling disputes, Bertrand Russell was dismissed from his fellowship of the University of Cambridge. Nevertheless, he escaped imprisonment, and continued to address public meetings up and down the country. At a meeting in the Houldsworth Hall, Manchester, with the Rev. Hewlett Johnson as chairman, Mr. Russell spoke about the significance of the Russian Revolution. In case of possible disorder a detachment of soldiers was in attendance. They became so interested in what Mr. Russell was saying that the officer in charge became afraid for their loyalty to King and Country, and marched them out.

Those of the anti-war movement refused to touch war, but could not stop war touching them. They would let war alone, but discovered that war would not let them alone. They went one step further than the hundreds of thousands of those who also hated to wage war, but saw it as their painful duty, a duty arising out of unchristian circumstances, the unchristian result of unchristian living, but a duty just the same. They of the anti-war movement were extremists and non-conformists, and like extremists and non-conformists all down the ages paid the price of their extremism and non-conformity, sometimes with life itself.

Chapter 7

THE BRITISH WORKING MAN

"The primary demand of labour today is not only an economic, but a human need. The operatives demand recognition by employers and managers that they are intelligent human beings—men and women—and not so many cogs in the industrial machine."

The speaker was an up-and-coming Trade Unionist called Ernest Bevin, and he was talking to a conference of Bristol employers and Trade Unionists in 1917. Mr. Bevin pleaded the cause of millions of decent, hardworking, respectable people whose lives were spent in drab and dreary surroundings. He was pleading for the rights of those who toiled long hours, for meagre wages, in factories, mines, shops, offices and in the fields. Formal education had ended at the age of twelve for many of them. They were that great, often inarticulate, mass of people over whom John Burns, that doughty champion of the poor, lamented, "The tragedy of the British working man is the poverty of his desires." All too often the intelligence, of which Mr. Bevin spoke, had little or no chance to develop, and life was accordingly the poorer and the more frustrated.

At the top of the affluence scale, in 1914, were the 13,850 people with incomes of over £5,000 per year, followed by the 47,000 whose annual incomes were in the £2,000 to £5,000 group. Many of the 338,000 professional men—doctors, lawyers and some clergymen—earned more than £1,000 a year, 400,000 salaried men earned more than £160 a year, the lowest figure upon which income tax was assessed. For all these men and their families a greater or less degree of gracious living was possible. In those days the prospect of a thousand a year, in addition to a handsome husband, was enough to rejoice the heart of most girls!

At the bottom end of the affluence scale were the 15,500,000 wage earners and the 1,200,000 self-employed small shop-keepers, hawkers and dressmakers. The men earned, on average, 25/9d per week, and the women 10/10½d. They harboured the perfectly reasonable desires for economic security, the right to work continuously for reasonably good wages, with the prospect of advancement, together with the desire to be treated as human beings, not just as "hands", as Mr. Bevin pointed out. But full and gracious living was only for the few in 1914, hence in large degree the seething discontent among British working men. Add to this the fact that the cost of living had been rising since the turn of the century, and wages had not kept pace with the increase in prices. When war came the Trade Unions were planning substantial demands for increases in wages, and de-creases in the number of hours worked. They were drawing up a constitution for a Triple Alliance of railwaymen, miners and transport workers, a plan not ratified until 1917. A social revolution was steadily building up.

Then came the war, and the Trade Unions had to re-think their position. On 24th August, 1914, the day the British troops began their historic retreat from Mons, the Trade Unions and the Labour Party leaders declared a truce with employers and managers. They would postpone their demands for improved wages and conditions until the end of the war, then confidently expected to take place at an early date, possibly by Christmas 1914. But the weeks and the months went by, with no sign of a quick and happy issue from Britain's afflictions. The govern-ment took the situation firmly in hand, and passed a series of defence regulations to deal with the emergency.

Under the Defence of the Realm Act the government took upon itself compulsory powers to commandeer any factory required for war work, and to issue directions to workers employed there. Strikes were declared unlawful, and disputes must be referred to arbitration. This Defence of the Realm Act was most comprehensive in its many clauses. It also covered matters like spreading false news, or any talk or action likely to discourage recruiting. In his leisure hours the British working man was wise to control his tongue. One East Londoner was fined £100 for remarking: "We shall see the Germans in the Mile End Road yet." Another British working man was heavily fined after being heard to express the opinion that "The King is a b . . . German." The Act permitted the opening and reading of suspicious looking letters. A garrulous letter about Hendon aerodrome cost an Edgware man a £100 fine. Reference has already been made, in an earlier chapter, to Clause 27c of the Act, requiring all writing about the war to be submitted to the Censor. Any writing about the war which did not put the whole blame on Germany was forbidden publication.

The Munitions of War Act, passed in July, 1915, made it a penal offence for a workman to leave his place of employment for another, without first gaining his employer's permission. To refuse a new job, at a lower wage or piece rate, or to refuse to work overtime, whether or not for extra pay, were likewise penal offences. However low his wage, the worker must not leave, even after giving notice, nor seek another job in another munitions factory. To make sure that these conditions were fulfilled it was decreed that no employer should employ a worker who could not produce a leaving certificate from his former employer. From the government angle all this was very businesslike, and well meant. But by July, 1915, food prices had risen 33 per cent above the August, 1914, level. Unfortunately wages had not! To do the government justice they had agreed in February, 1915, to war bonuses to railwaymen. Those whose weekly wage did not exceed 30/- were awarded an extra 3/-. The relatively affluent ones whose wage exceeded £1.10-0 had to be content with an extra 2/-.

Strikes were illegal for the duration, were they? Hardly had the Act been passed than the South Wales miners, 200,000 of them, "came out". Since the Royal Navy depended upon them for coal an early settlement was essential. Lloyd George hastened to South Wales, and settled the strike on the miners' own terms. The Clyde engineers were the next to strike. The government, from that time onwards, pursued a policy of wages advances in the form of "war bonuses", which left real wages well below the 1914 level, as prices steadily advanced. By November, 1918, food prices had increased by 133 per cent above the August, 1914, level, and the cost of living as a whole by 125 per cent.

Strikes continued, spasmodically, for the duration of the war. 1917 was marked by much industrial unrest. In May strikes occurred at the munitions works in Sheffield, Barrow-in-Furness, London and Glasgow. In July, 1918, munitions workers struck at Birmingham and Coventry. Most alarming of all, to the government, was the strike of the London policemen, on 31st August, 1918. Lloyd George at once gave way to their demands, and several years later remarked : "This country was nearer to Bolshevism that day than at any time since."

The Russian Revolution, in March, 1917, occasioned great rejoicing. A monster demonstration on May Day that year closed down work on Clydeside. In June a convention was held in Leeds with the object of establishing a nationwide network of Workers' and Soldiers' Councils, on the Bolshevik pattern. The government was not unduly alarmed by the Leeds conference. They regarded it as a useful safety valve for the extremist views of such groups as the Independent Labour Party, the British Socialist Party, the Union of Democratic Control and the National Council of Civil Liberties, none of whom supported the war effort. In the event the government proved right. Nothing came of the grandiose scheme for Councils of Soldiers and

Workmen. Lower Deck Committees were organised in some ships of the Royal Navy based on the south coast, but no signs of mutiny were reported.

Firms engaged in war work asked for the return of 50,000 skilled mechanics from the Army. In spite of indignant opposition from the military authorities 40,000 men were returned to civilian life. Many of these men felt that they were running away from danger and hardship into safety, comfort and affluence. They had to cross the great gulf which had opened between soldiers and the civilians for whom they were daily risking their lives. The men at the Front felt a certain sympathy for the Germans, men like themselves flung into the furnace of war. At home the returned mechanics found a general mood of hatred, malice and all uncharitableness against the Germans, a mood sustained by propaganda displaying the Allies as angels of light, and the enemy as devils.

The wartime factories also saw the rise to power of the shop stewards. Before the war they were minor officials who checked up on cards and dues for their union. When war came they were asked by their workmates to present grievances to the management. In addition to taking up grievances reported to them, they themselves actively sought out untoward happenings in their workshops. In 1916 their activities were co-ordinated in the National Shop Stewards and Workers' Committee Movement.

Britain depended for victory not only upon the factory workers, but also upon those who worked in agriculture. According to the 1911 census 21.9 per cent of the population lived in rural areas. The National Agricultural Wages Board, set up in 1917, had power to fix wages in each area, acting on the advice of the Local Wages Committees of farmers and labourers. They conceded a minimum wage of 25/-, against the demands of the Labour Party and the Trade Unions for 30/-. By the end of the war this meagre sum had risen to 30/6d. The depleted numbers of agricultural workers—depleted by the call-up—were supplemented by the autumn of 1918 by 30,000 German prisoners-of-war. Few of these Germans even wanted, much less attempted, to escape. They were content to work, and to be under the supervision of the local police.

Much of the responsibility for maintaining the war effort in the factories fell upon Mr. Lloyd George, when he was appointed Minister of Munitions, in 1915. He realised that much of the unrest among the workers was caused by the huge profits made by firms engaged in war work. Nevertheless he showed much skill in settling disputes and in persuading the workers to great efforts. He was well received in one Lancashire munitions factory, where he asked for a quarter of a million shells a month. He was promised a million before long, and the workers' only complaint was that they wished they had been told eight months before!

But his visits to the munitions works did not always work out so smoothly and harmoniously. He discovered that, to his responsibility for what he called "the terrible task of manufacturing engines for human mutilation and slaughter" there was added the possibilities of conflicts with the Trade Unions over matters of hours, wages and the mixing of skilled and unskilled labour. Christmas Eve, 1915, found him travelling with Arthur Henderson to Glasgow, there to deal with a disturbance which interfered with the delivery of big guns. On arrival they summoned the shop stewards, to acquaint them with the exact position, and to ask their help in stimulating production. The leader of the shop stewards, David Kirkwood, responded by lecturing Mr. Lloyd George and Mr. Henderson on the subject of the degrading state of servitude in which they lived and laboured.

"I am as much a slave of Sir William Beardsmore" (this was Beardsmore's factory), "as if I had the letter B branded on my brow," declared Mr. Kirkwood. Among other workers' leaders in Glasgow Mr. Lloyd George and Mr. Henderson also met a Mr. William Gallagher, a well-mannered and smooth-spoken Communist whom Mr. Lloyd George regarded as the most sinister influence of all among the Clyde engineers. After this unpromising beginning the workers gathered in St. Andrew's Hall, on Christmas morning, with Mr. Henderson in the chair of the meeting. In spite of a noisy minority who were against the two visitors having a fair hearing, the dispute was settled for the time, and there was a temporary improvement in production.

On most occasions Mr. Lloyd George's direct and reasonable approach was effective. He would compare the lot of the workers with the lot of their comrades in the trenches. "The enlisted workman cannot choose his locality of action," he reminded them. "He cannot say, 'I am quite prepared to fight at Neuve Chapelle, but I won't fight at Festubert, and I am not going to the place they call Wipers.' He cannot say, 'I have been in the trenches $8\frac{1}{2}$ hours, and my Trade Union won't allow me to work more than 8 hours.'"

When the munitions workers of Coventry and Birmingham struck in July, 1918, they were reminded that if they did not return to work they were liable to be called up for military service. They had been granted exemption because their services were considered more valuable in the workshop than in the trenches. Faced with this unpalatable alternative the strikers lost no time in returning to their workshops. Addressing Trade Union leaders at a conference on manpower, in January, 1918, Mr. Lloyd George, who was then Prime Minister, told them bluntly: "Do not let us harbour any delusions . . . you, the people, must either go on or go under."

Another formidable ally of the government, and friend of the British working man, was the journalist and financial operator, some time Member of Parliament (first as a Liberal, and then as an Independent) for South Hackney, founder of the *Financial Times,* founder and first editor of *John Bull,* Mr. Horatio William Bottomley. As a maker of recruiting speeches he had few, if any, equals. Having persuaded many to enlist, he also identified himself wholeheartedly with the cause of the common soldier. This inevitably involved him with the British working men in the factories and fields, upon whom the soldier depended for arms and food. On the platform and in the press he adopted the tactics of the "heart to heart chat" to miners, engineers, railway-men, and munitions workers. His approach was "man to man, brother to brother—aye, and may I say it, worker to worker. I really don't think any one works harder than I do." His technique was one of "sympathetic attention, which only full mutual trust could engender. Put yourself in their place, and speak in language they can understand."

Working on such sound psychological principles Mr. Bottom-ley could hardly fail to make a substantial contribution to the solution of Britain's industrial problems. In a typical article, published in the *Sunday Pictorial* in May, 1917, he wrote:

"So come, boys, let's have a confab. Your brother, your boy, in the trenches, is having the devil of a time. He has all sorts of real, grim grievances, but not a word of complaint escapes his lips. And as for striking. . . . !" Words failed even Mr. Bottomley at the very suggestion of a strike at such a time of crisis in our rough island story. He went on to explain why:

"A strike today is an affront to the patriotism of the Empire, a blasphemy against our holy cause. A man who downs tools is an enemy to King and Country. Put yourself in the place of your son or pal in the trenches, when ammunition runs out. Can you see him falling, mortally wounded, writhing in agony, with a curse for the strikers on his lips? While we sleep peacefully in our beds the guns are booming in a ceaseless cacophony of terror. Then at dawn, over the top they go, heroes all. Not a footstep wavers, not a man is afraid."

All this was good, rousing stuff, but in a confab with the boys in the factories there was another matter which could not be ignored. That was the high profits being made by employers—the hard-faced men who were doing very well out of the war. This undisputed, ugly fact lay at the heart of much of the resentment and unrest in the mind of the British working man. Neither Mr. Bottomley, nor any one else, could ignore this fact if progress towards greater production was to be made. Mr. Bottomley first apologised for his blunt words about strikers. "I am sorry to have to speak so plainly, but you will respect me all the more for doing so." Then he proceeded to try to grasp the nettle of the war profiteers.

"Employers who impose harsh conditions on workers, endeavour to line their filthy pockets with blood-stained gold . . . may their souls writhe in hell for their villainy! If I had my way 50 per cent of all Excess Profits due to war work would be distributed among the men. That is the way to avoid strikes!"

It was indeed, but as Mr. Bottomley, and every thoughtful reader knew quite well, there was not the remotest chance of this suggestion being put into operation.

So what? In the circumstances Mr. Bottomley could only write feelingly: "In spite of this, think of our brave soldiers and sailors, uncomplaining. Can you be less self-sacrificing and enduring than our brothers on sea and land? Come lads, can't you trust at least some of us to see the debt due to you by a grateful State shall be paid in full? I implore you to postpone all your troubles until the boys are safe. Stand by the boys at the Front!" Mr. Bottomley concluded: "Stick to your work! Play the man—the big, brave man on whose back the Empire rests!"

So the hard-faced men went on doing very well out of the war, and the workers sustained themselves with the hope that some day the grateful State would settle in full the debt owed to the big, brave men on whose backs the Empire rested. The editor of the *Sunday Pictorial* backed up by Mr. Bottomley's eloquent and rousing plea with his "Sunday Thought", on this occasion an apt quotation from the writings of Marcus Aurelius: "Let it make do difference to thee whether thou art cold or warm, if thou art doing thy duty."

When Mr. Lloyd George became Prime Minister he was succeeded at the Ministry of Munitions by Mr. Winston Churchill, who at once began to streamline the organisation. 50 departments were reduced to 10, and a daily General Council Meeting was inaugurated under Mr. Churchill's presidency. Within six months the strength of the Tank Corps was increased by 27 per cent, production of machine guns by 41 per cent, and the number of aeroplanes in France by 40 per cent.

From time to time the British public was reminded that the soldiers in the trenches were not the only ones to live dangerously. The munitions workers, men and women, also lived under the daily threat of being blown to pieces. North London was made aware of this on 9th January, 1917, when the Silvertown munitions factory blew up, 69 people were killed, 400 people were injured, and hundreds were rendered homeless by the violence of the explosion, which severely damaged nearby streets as well as the factory itself. Chilwell, in Nottinghamshire, was the scene of another spectacular explosion, accompanied by widespread damage and loss of life. The national shell filling factory there provided over 19 million shells, just over 50 per cent of those used by the British Army, during the course of the war. On 1st July, 1918, a great explosion caused 134 deaths. The men who daily risked their lives in munitions factories were paid a flat rate of £2/19/3d per week, which war bonuses brought to £4/6/6d. Foremen received £5/1/10d.

War brought full employment to Britain. Vendors of matches and boot laces disappeared from the streets for the duration. Trade Union membership increased from 2¼ millions in 1913, to 4½ millions in 1918. The employers banded together, in 1916, in the Federation of British Industries. Strikes were relatively few—or we should never have won the war. Many would-be strikers were deterred by the threat of the call-up. Sustained by the hope of some great social improvement arising from the ashes of war, the British working man, in field and factory, like Mr. H. G. Wells' Mr. Britling, "saw it through".

Chapter 8

THE BRITISH WORKING WOMAN

THE old proverb reminds us that it is an ill wind that blows no one any good. The Great War was a wind that blew grievous ill to multitudes of women, when their husbands, sons, brothers and sweethearts were killed or maimed. But that, as we shall see, was not the whole story. For a great many women war was also the great liberator.

Reference has already been made, in the opening chapter, to the arduous and dreary conditions under which housewives, in town and country, lived and laboured, in the second decade of the twentieth century. They carried on without benefit of so many household labour-saving gadgets commonplace in the second half of the century. They were born too soon to enjoy the advantages of the electric washer, the spin drier, the electric iron, the kitchen range. In the absence of vacuum cleaners, carpets drier; oil, gas or electric central heating, bathroom and indoor toilet.

For them the weekly washing day meant rising up early in the morning, lighting the copper fire, scrubbing the clothes and then putting them through the hand-turned mangle, all in an atmosphere heavy with steam and the smell of "Sunlight" soap. If the weather was fine, the clothes were dried in the backyard; if wet, hung on a pulley in the kitchen to dry from the heat of the vacuum cleaner, the refrigerator, the food mixer, the hair and mats were taken into the backyard, to have the dust beaten out of them. Gas stoves, but not electric stoves, were quite commoon, though the kitchen range was still extensively used for cooking and for heating water. In town or country a bath, usually taken before the kitchen fire, was a major operation. It involved a re-organisation of the family comings and goings, as well as heating sufficient water. Small wonder that when Sunday afternoon came along, after a strenuous week of scrubbing, sweeping, baking, sewing, darning and shopping, the housewife was only too glad to put up her weary feet for an hour, after packing off the children to Sunday School, partly for their spiritual good, and partly for the sake of temporary peace and quiet in the house.

Many of the daughters of the poor, on reaching the age of 14, began to earn their living in domestic service. Wages for maids ranged from £13 per year upwards, with "keep", uniform, laundry, and in the larger houses, the use of the servants' hall in their scanty leisure moments. In the manufacturing towns of the north country many girls and women were employed in the cotton and woollen mills. 80,000 country women and girls worked on the land. Others, looking for more genteel ways of earning their keep, became school teachers, or found employment in offices as "typewriters", as they were quaintly called. Yet others became "nannies" to the children of the affluent, or became nurses in hospitals and infirmaries.

The daughters of gentlemen tended to be looked upon as domestic ornaments. No lady entered the kitchen, except to issue orders. The more thoughtful ones were already rebellious against the empty, useless lives convention expected them to lead. The social round, interspersed by such good works as selling "Alexandra roses" for the benefit of the hospitals, did not satisfy an increasing number of the thinking young women of 1914. H. G. Wells caught this spirit of rebellion in his novel *Ann Veronica*, published in 1909, and viewed with grave disapproval by old fashioned, disciplinarian parents. Many of these young rebels joined the Suffragette movement, where they found a cause to

66

serve, namely "Votes for women". In the furtherance of this cause they suffered sometimes unnecessarily rough handling from stewards in meetings from which they were ejected, and later imprisonment and forcible feeding.

Then came the war. As political prisoners suffragettes were released from gaol. Only a minority of suffragettes declared against women playing their part in the war effort. They were led by Miss Sylvia Pankhurst and Mrs. Despard, sister of Sir John French, the leader of the British Expeditionary Force. But the National Union of Women's Suffrage Societies and the Women's Social and Political Union called a truce with the authorities, and placed themselves unreservedly behind the war effort. Baroness Orczy, the novelist, creator of the *Scarlet Pimpernel,* founded the Women of England's Active Service League, with the object of persuading men to enlist at the nearest recruiting station. They claimed 20,000 successful persuasions, out of the 100,000 at which they aimed. Women and girls were also enlisted in the White Feather movement, launched in a patriotic speech by Admiral Penrose Fitzgerald, made from the bandstand, on the front at Folkestone. The idea was to jog the conscience of young men still in civilian clothes, by handing them a white feather. No statistics exist to tell how effective this proved as a method of recruitment.

By the early months of 1915 there were signs that a great revolution in the conventional thinking about women's place in society was well under way. More than a million men had by then responded to the call to arms, leaving all those places to fill in commerce, industry and the public services, not to mention the demands for an ever increasing amount of armaments to win the war. A Conservative M.P. named Walter Long declared: "There are still places where women believe their place is in the home. That idea must be met, and combated."

There followed a massive recruitment of women to help their menfolk win the war. When war broke out 14,000 workers were employed at Woolwich Arsenal. By 1916 the number employed at Woolwich and its satellite factories was 100,000, and 50,000 of them were women. By June, 1917, most of the machine work on shells, fuses and trench warfare supplies was done by women. They worked long hours, in highly dangerous conditions, for a wage which war bonuses had raised by 1918 to £2/2/4d per week. Several hundreds died in explosions, notably at Silvertown and Chilwell. Others died of pernicious anaemia contracted by handling high explosive powder. Others suffered eczema, from handling TNT, the fumes from which could also cause symptoms resembling pneumonia or jaundice. Yet others were nicknamed "Canaries", because the explosives among which they worked turned their complexions a bright yellow. Mrs. Pankhurst told of women in a London aircraft works, engaged in painting aeroplane wings with a varnish that gave off toxic fumes. When Mrs. Pankhurst visited this factory she found six out of the thirty women engaged in one workshop lying outside, recovering from the effects of the poisonous atmosphere in which they worked. Just as there were youths who lied about their age in order to enlist in the army, so there were young girls who made themselves out to be older than they were in order to "do their bit" in the munition factories. One of these was 17-year-old Mabel Lethbridge. She volunteered for work in a hut where high explosives were poured and packed into shells. A device known as a "monkey machine" forced a mixture of amotol and TNT into 18" shell cases. Four girls hauled on a rope to raise a huge weight which they let fall on to the mixture to pack it tightly. Towards the end of the shift there was a tremendous explosion, Mabel was the sole survivor, and she lay unconscious for ten days. Her left leg was amputated, and during the next fifty years she endured forty-five operations. Her grateful country awarded her the C.B.E.

As the war dragged on, and the area of conflict widened, Woolwich Arsenal expanded until it covered nine square miles. The 30,000 women workers were under the care and direction of a Lady Superintendent, Miss Lilian Barker, who in after years

Plate 5—Women police patrol collaborating with police
constable outside Euston Station.

(*Photo: Imperial War Museum.*)

Plate 6—Mechanics of the Womens' Royal Air Force working on the fuselage of an Avro biplane. (*Photo: Imperial War Museum.*)

did good service as Governor of the Borstal Institution at Ayles-bury. In order to maintain morale at the necessary high level Miss Barker drafted her "Thoughts for Munition Workers".

MOTIVE FOR WORK : PATRIOTISM. A munitions worker has as important a job as the soldier in the trenches, and on her his life depends.

AIM : OUTPUT. Anyone who limits this is a traitor to her sweet-heart, brother or husband who is fighting. One minute lost by sixty girls means the loss of one hour's output. This includes slacking at meals and at closing time.

HAPPINESS. If any worker does not like her job she should give it up. She will be of no use, and will probably be a bad influence.

Sustained by these forthright and challenging sentiments the girls worked twelve hour shifts, doing work that was often mono-tonous, arduous and sometimes dangerous.

More fortunate were those women and girls who took up the much healthier, and just as necessary form of national service, as land workers. As the submarine menace to our shipping mounted the necessity to grow more and more of our food be-came essential. The Women's Land Army, a mobile body of regular women land workers, came into being, organised by the Ministry of Agriculture. Free training, with maintenance, for a period of up to six weeks, was given to suitable applicants. The lady was then provided with free working kit, and a guaranteed minimum wage of 25/- per week. By August, 1918, nearly 16,000 of them were tilling the soil, and making a useful contribution to Britain's depleted food supplies. The Women's Land Army, together with a large number of part-time women workers, brought the total female contingent of agricultural workers up to 400,000. In the absence of so many men who had been drafted into the armed forces their contribution to the nation's survival was a vital one.

From the early days of the war it became increasingly apparent that the number of trained nurses in our hospitals was quite inadequate to deal with the appalling number of casualties at the Front. Years before the war bodies of civilians, men as well as women, had received some training under the Haldane scheme, organised by the British Red Cross Society and the St. John Ambulance Association. The idea was that, in an emergency, they should be ready and qualified to render first aid to the injured at a moment's notice. In October, 1914, the women decided to work together as Joint Women's Voluntary Aid Detachments, popularly know as V.A.D.s. Many thousands of them were attached to military hospitals, in Britain and overseas. They worked twelve hour shifts, nursing the wounded, for a monetary reward of £20 per year, plus their "keep", a uniform allowance, and the cost of laundering their clothes. 23,000 of them worked as nurses, and 15,000 as orderlies, sometimes in hospital wards that were no more than marquees.

41,000 women performed their part in maintaining the war effort by joining the Women's Army Auxiliary Corps, known as W.A.A.Cs. for short. Members enlisted for the duration of the war, and served as clerks, telephone operators, cooks, store women and in salvage and ambulance work, in connection with the British Army. 17,000 of them served abroad.

The Women's Royal Naval Service was established by the Admiralty to release Royal Naval personnel from shore duties. The 5,000 members were employed at naval bases as cooks, clerks, orderlies, drivers and storekeepers. Similar duties were performed on aerodromes, at home and abroad, by women who joined the Women's Auxiliary Air Force.

Another wartime development was the appearance of women police in the streets of towns and cities. The Criminal Law Amendment Committee had, for some time, been pressing for the appointment of women police to deal with cases involving women and girls. At first the Women Police Volunteers, which in 1915 became the Women's Police Service, was a full-time body of uniformed police women dependent upon voluntary donations. In 1916, the government, realising the value of the work they were doing, made a grant for their support. The members were trained in First Aid, police court procedure and ju-jitsu. Britain's first uniformed policewoman was Mary Sophia Allen, a former suffragette who knew the inside of a gaol, after she was sentenced for trying to force her way into the Houses of Parliament. She died in 1964, aged 86. Grantham was the first town to avail itself of the services of the women police. The presence of 18,000 troops on the outskirts of the town brought its own peculiar social problems, when drink and girls were almost the only source of entertainment for the soldiery. Two policewomen began their patrols in the town. They kept vigilant watch on dark passages, alleys, shop doorways and public houses. They arrested drunken and disorderly women. But where the objects of their attention retained their sober senses the policewomen relied on reasonable-ness, allied to firmness. Girls who seemed to be in moral danger were visited in their homes, and talked to in a natural manner about the dangers of loitering about in the vicinity of army camps. The policewomen rendered notable service at Gretna, where the government had established extensive munitions works. They visited the factories and hostels, and broke up street brawls. 150 policewomen were regularly engaged in searching female workers, to prevent any forbidden articles being taken into the workshops. In London, and other large centres of population, they engaged in moral welfare patrols, after dark. The London Strand was a particularly notorious area for prostitutes plying their trade, and was nick-named by the policewomen "The Devil's Promenade". Dressed in their dark blue uniforms, leather-belted tunics, long, heavy skirts, and hard felt hats the police-women played their notable part in preserving law and order, and in preventing even more lechery in the permissive atmosphere of wartime Britain.

Other women acted as drivers and conductresses on buses and trams, delivered the mail, lit the street lamps, acted as porters at railway stations, kept accounts, in fact engaged in most jobs open to men with the exception of mining and building. 400,000 of the women who replaced men called up for war service were domestic servants, for whom the war provided an escape route from working conditions that were sometimes not far removed from slavery. Housewives who did not "go out to work" also played their part in maintaining the war effort, by various forms of service during their leisure hours. Women's Institutes appeared in many villages. This organisation of countrywomen was started by farmers' wives in Canada, in 1897.

The first Women's Institute in Britain was formed in 1915, by a Canadian lady, Mrs. Alfred Watt, in the village of Llanfairpwllgwyngyll, Anglesey. The movement, democratic, nonpolitical and non-sectarian, spread rapidly until there were enough branches to form the National Federation of Women's Institutes in 1917. The Ministry of Agriculture and Fisheries recognising the value of the institutes in helping and teaching countrywomen to maintain food supplies, made a small annual grant to the running expenses. The institutes were, and still are, limited to villages and small rural towns.

All over the country church halls were opened for canteen and recreational facilities for troops stationed, or passing through the area—another widespread form of voluntary wartime service for the women who staffed them. In towns where large numbers of troops were billeted, or encamped, the canteens, with their facilities for light refreshments and games, formed a valuable counter-attraction to the public house. Others, sited near large railway stations, offered welcome refreshment to the traveller passing that way. For instance, many a soldier, with an hour or more to wait for his train at Preston, Lancashire, was glad of the plate of wholesome porridge available at the nearby Lune Street Wesleyan Church canteen.

Many thousands of kindly, motherly souls spent hours knitting scarves, socks, balaclava helmets, gloves and other comforts for the troops. All these, and many other essential services to the nation by women were rightly and properly recognised in the last year of the war, 1918. The way in which women had not only ministered to the wounded, but had also enabled industry to carry on, pleaded the right of woman to vote much more convincingly than the antics and outrages of the suffragettes. In February, 1918, women of thirty years of age and over were given the right to vote. Another decade was to pass before the age was lowered to twenty-one.

For good, as well as for ill, the winds of change had blown through the lives of the women of Britain during the years of the world conflict. Evidence for this was to be seen in the changes wrought in the outward appearance of women. They had been liberated from tight lacing, from enormous hats, long trailing skirts and great masses of hair. Long hair and long skirts were a hindrance, and sometimes a positive danger, on the factory floor. When some poor women had been scalped, through their hair becoming entangled in factory machinery, crowning glory or no crowning glory, "bobbed" hair was obviously the practical fashion to adopt in time of war.

For the first time great numbers of women had worked outside their own homes, and had shown themselves to be capable of being self-supporting and independent. Some of them had actually gone to distant towns, and worked a hundred miles, or more, from their homes. They had received regular wages, and been praised by the highest in the land, for the work they did. In their social life they had dispensed with chaperones, had "gone out with the boys" to theatres, music halls, cinemas, pubs and clubs, and learned to smoke and to swear. Never again would they be content to be looked upon as the inferiors of men, or to be regarded as merely domestic ornaments or domestic drudges. War, the great destroyer, was for women also the great liberator. The process of liberation had begun before the war. The peculiar circumstances of wartime Britain greatly accelerated that process.

Chapter 9

CHILDREN

WHAT was it like to be a small boy, of working class parentage, growing up in wartime England between 1914 and 1918? Here are the personal recollections of a child of that time, living in the industrial north of England.

"I was born, and grew up, in the drab and dreary, smoky and smelly town called Widnes, in south Lancashire. The principal industries were the manufacture of chemicals and soap. In those early years of the twentieth century Widnes was variously described as 'a veritable helltown,' 'a metropolis of smells,' and as 'renowned for good soap and bad smells.' " True, on the rising ground to the north of the rows and rows of terraced houses which formed the main bulk of the town, there were green fields and a park. But these living conditions were not for the great majority of the residents of Widnes. We lived on the eastern edge of the town. When we looked out of the front windows we saw a drab railway station, flanked by a piece of waste ground, beyond which were rows of terraced houses built in the 1860s, to house the workers in the nearby chemical factory. Looking out of the side windows we saw railway lines, and beyond them a chemical works. From no window was it possible to feast the eyes upon a tree, a flower or even a blade of grass. According to rumour the chemical works now manufactured, among other things, poison gas. Whether this was true, or not, the vile smells issuing from

74

them bade fair to poison us!

My two brothers and I received the first part of our formal education at an elementary school (as they were then called), which stood about three quarters of a mile away from where we lived. There we were well grounded in reading, writing, arithmetic and Bible stories. In addition to this we also learned a lot about the wicked Germans, and their despicable Kaiser. They had shot Nurse Cavell, sunk the *Lusitania* and many food ships, were daily killing our brave boys with poison gas, and killing women and children, as well as men, by dropping bombs on England from their Zeppelins. We also learned about 16-year-old sailor boy, Jack Cornwell, who was killed in the Battle of Jutland. Although mortally wounded early in the fight, with the gun's crew lying dead and dying around him, he remained standing at an exposed post, awaiting orders. He was posthumously awarded the V.C. This story was used to persuade us to bring our pennies to be invested in War Savings. Those who did so received a little album in which to stick coloured stamps bearing pictures of Jack Cornwell's end, and of other war scenes.

One aspect of this war propaganda rather puzzled me. The books we used in our reading lessons were published before the war. One of them contained a chapter about Germany, illustrated with a picture of a German family engaged in the pleasant and peaceful business of gathering cherries in an orchard. A buxom, motherly looking woman, and three or four rosy cheeked children stood at the foot of a cherry tree, looking up expectantly. Father, an ordinary looking man, with a large moustache, and who reminded me of one of my uncles, was up among the branches about to hand down a bunch of cherries. Really! Just what kind of people were these Germans? It was all very puzzling to a boy of seven! Did I ask teacher to explain? No. The thought never crossed my mind. We also learned a number of patriotic songs, in addition to ditties like: *Sweet and Low, The Bay of Biscay* and *The Golden Vanity*. Although hardly any of us had even seen, much less sailed the sea, we sang with

75

great gusto: *Rule Britannia, Ye Mariners of England, Britannia the pride of the ocean,* and *Hearts of Oak.* We also sang *Three Cheers for the Red, White and Blue,* and a song whose title now eludes me, something about "Fighting for glory, or a soldier's grave".

Before we left school for home, in the late afternoon, we lifted up our infant voices in the prayer:

> Lord keep us safe this night,
> Secure from all our fears.
> May angels guard us while we sleep,
> Till morning light appears.

Then, on wintry days, we hastened home in the gathering gloom. The street lamps were unlit, in conformity with wartime regulations, but the lamp-posts were painted white to prevent our bumping into them in the dark. In the smoky atmosphere of Widnes they did not remain white for long. When darkness came the skies were stabbed by the light of searchlights. An anti-aircraft gun stood in a farmyard on the edge of the town, an additional reassurance that the authorities had our safety at heart. German aircraft approached the town only on one occasion, in the early hours of the morning one day in April, 1918. The gas supply was turned off at the local gasworks. plunging the whole town into total darkness.

Bombs were dropped to the north of the town. The sole casualty was a milestone, scarred by bomb splinters. This milestone was uprooted from its place beside the highway, and transferred to a flower bed in the park. There it stood, with a plaque describing the occasion, a mute witness to the air raid damage susained by Widnes during the Great War. We went on Sundays to a large Wesleyan Chapel. I was too small to follow the sermons preached there, but certain hymns, which expressed the feelings and aspirations of the people were, I remember, sung frequently, led by a fine choir and pipe organ. One of them ran :—

76

Plate 7—Women war workers on axle sub-assembly in engineering workshops, 1917. (*Photo: Hulton Picture Library.*)

Plate 8—Women war workers assembling a lorry in engineering workshops, 1917.
(Photo: Hulton Picture Library.)

Break, day of God, O break!
The earth with strife is worn,
The hills with thunder shake,
Hearts of the people mourn.
Break, day of God, sweet day of peace,
And bid the shout of warriors cease.

Something of the earnestness and the fervour with which those words were sung communicated itself to the 7-year-old boy joining in with his piping voice.

Would my father be called up? For many months there was considerable doubt about this. He was a railwayman, head carter, and for many years a familiar figure in the streets of Widnes, with his horse and dray, delivering goods to the shops. He was 38 years of age when war broke out, and passed as physically A1. He attested under the Derby scheme described in an earlier chapter. Finally, after much wrangling between the representatives of the railway and the military authorities, he was exempted as indispensable. Railwaymen were very poorly paid, but they were given a limited number of free passes, and unlimited opportunities of privilege travel at a quarter of the normal fare, for themselves and their families. We were therefore able to escape from Widnes, for a week every year, to rural Lincolnshire. My parents were Lincolnshire people, and our relations still lived in that county. My father came to Widnes in 1898, when he took employment as a railwayman, and left agricultural work. How we enjoyed that long train journey! From Widnes to Lincoln the going was good, no long waits on stations, and that thrilling three miles of near darkness when the train passed through the Woodhead tunnel. But at Lincoln we had a two hours wait for the Boston train. We explored the city, being suitably impressed and awed by the great cathedral. One poignant memory of war-time Lincoln was the benches at intervals in the streets, labelled "For wounded soldiers only", and often occupied by blue uniformed men, some with an arm or leg missing. Then we boarded

77

the Boston train, and crawled along through Five Mile House
Tattersal, Dogdyke and Langrick, into Boston where we had
another two hours wait until the Skegness train took us on the
last stage of our journey. First Sibsey, then Old Leake and a
last, Eastville (for New Leake), where my grandmother lived.

During the holiday we always had one day at nearby Skegness
When we left the pure air of Lincolnshire for the impure air o
Widnes, my mother would remark proudly: "Not many boy
at your school have been as far as you have this holidaytime!"

As the war dragged on food presented a growing problem. A
breakfast we had oatmeal porridge. At dinnertime (we called th
midday meal "dinner", not "lunch"), we eked out our miserabl
meat ration with the aid of tasty Foster Clark's soups
oxtail and mock turtle being the favourites. My mother regarde
the coarse cuts of meat supplied to us with a suspicious eye, an
declared they were horseflesh. Rice pudding, sometimes boile
rice, figured so prominently on the menu that I swore a silen
oath that when I was older I would never touch the stuff agai
—an oath I have kept to this day. Our health was maintained b
doses of liquorice powder, and when our strength needed build
ing up after the usual childish ailments, the doctor ordered u
Parrish's Chemical Food, and Cod Liver Oil and Malt. As suga
was in short supply we tried saccharine tablets as a sweetener—
but only once! We found them horrible!

By way of outdoor recreation we bowled our hoops, spun ou
tops, and played marbles and pitching cigarette cards, in additio
to simple ball games. We collected cigarette cards, aiming t
complete the whole "pack" of a given series. I was at a disad
vantage here, as my father was a non-smoker. We read all th
comics we could lay hands upon. *Funny Wonder, Chips, Com*
Cuts were all priced at ½d. when the war began, but soon double
in price. *Funny Wonder* was my favourite, as the front pag
bore a strip featuring Charlie Chaplin. We also read *Rainbo*
(with the adventures of Tiger Tim on the front page), *Puc*
Chuckles and the *Sunday Fairy*. The last-named wa

78

recommended for children's Sunday reading because the back page featured some Bible story told in pictures. My older brother read *Magnet, Gem, Penny Popular, Sexton Blake Library* and *Boys' Own Paper*. I also liked to read the *Penny Pictorial,* which became the *Pictorial Magazine* when the price went up to 2d. In addition to lots of pictures this magazine also contained stories about the exploits of a detective called Derwent Duff, which introduced me to the pleasures of reading "whodunnits", a pleasure that has remained with me down the years. We did not buy all these publications. A great deal of "swapping" was done, and kind friends passed on others when they had finished with them. On wet, wintry days we stayed indoors and played dominoes, snakes and ladders, Ludo, Snap and learned how to play draughts. We had our toys, too. I graduated from wooden and tin model railway engines to a set of wooden building blocks, toy soldiers and a realistic model of a French .75 gun, which fired little wooden missiles.

The 30,000 odd inhabitants of Widnes were served in those days, for entertainment purposes, by three cinemas, a theatre and a music hall that interspersed acts with short films. On our occasional visits to the cinema we saw some of the early Chaplin comedies, and one Pearl White in a serial called *The House of Hate,* in which she weekly escaped a fate worse than death at the hands of the Hooded Terror. How we shouted: "Hey-up!" to her as the hooded one crept up stealthily behind her! This was at a cinema with the unique name of the Bozzadrome, after the nickname of the proprietor, "Bozza" Martin. This cinema was locally known, not without justification, as the "Bughouse", as well as "Bozzas" for short.

In those days the welfare services were beginning to deal adequately with the problems of children who lived below, or just above, the poverty line. In the depths of winter some poor children still came to school barefooted, without overcoats, and in dirty, ragged clothes. Some came breakfastless, too. Lice in the hair was a common problem. My mother ensured that we were kept free from this nuisance by regularly going through our hair with a fine comb. Ringworm and rickets were two other health problems. Just how much of these problems were due to primary poverty, and how much to secondary poverty (the wrong use of money), and to neglect, the sociologists do not appear to have yet discovered. In some instances the pay packets of the fathers of these unfortunate children were as heavy as my father's. My brothers and I were always adequately clothed, shod and fed, in spite of my father's low wage as a railwayman. The reason was twofold. My parents were good managers where money was concerned, and they also observed the good Wesleyan teaching whereby not one single penny of their hard earned money went to either the publican or the bookie.

The war, with its alarms, its sorrows and its shortages at last came to an end. On the dull November Monday morning, 11th November, 1918, we sat in school waiting expectantly for the hour of eleven. Teacher had told us how, one after another Bulgaria, Turkey, Austria and now Germany had collapsed and the old Kaiser had run away to Holland. Eleven o'clock! The factory sirens sounded! "The war's over, boys! Half holiday this afternoon!" said teacher, jubilantly. Loud cheers from us boys, as much for the half holiday as for the end of the war."

We have seen, in the foregoing reminiscences, that the typical child fared reasonably well amid the stringencies and dangers of wartime Britain. Classes were large, anything from forty to sixty scholars in each class in the elementary schools. But discipline was strict, though seldom harsh, and the child who really wanted to learn could do so, though the teaching methods might seem crude in our days. In many homes the Victorian attitude of deferring to parents still prevailed, though very, very few children still addressed father as "Sir". The great majority still left school when they reached the age of 14. The boys then donned long trousers. Previously they had worn either knickerbockers, or shorts that covered the knees, over long black stockings.

The aristocratic boys who were educated at public schools, like Eton, Harrow, Uppingham and others, wore long trousers, short jackets and stiff, white "Eton" collars. The great majority of children attended Council schools, set up by the local School Boards in 1870, and the years following. Absent scholars were visited in their homes by the school attendance officer, or "the School Board man", as he was called, to ascertain the real reason for their non-attendance.

Brighter children in the elementary schools had the opportunity of "winning a scholarship" which entitled them, at the age of 11, to receive education at a Secondary or Grammar School, where the minimum school leaving age was 16. 25 per cent of the places in these Secondary Schools were reserved for "scholarship", or non-fee paying students. But they had to buy their own textbooks, either new, or at secondhand from those who had outgrown them. Classes were usually numerically smaller than in the elementary schools, though thirty or thirty-five to the class was quite usual. There the brighter child could matriculate, then pass his Higher School Certificate examinations and qualify for a university course, again with the help of a scholarship. The majority left at the age of 16, either with his School Certificate of Education, with passes at "Credit" level in up to four subjects, or better still Matriculation, with "Credit" level passes in at least five subjects. The call-up of men brought its problems to all schools. The situation was met by married women returning to their former profession, and by retired teachers making a return for the duration of the war.

In 1916 the historian, Mr. H. A. L. Fisher, was appointed President of the Board of Education, a landmark in the history of education in Britain. His Education Act, which became law in 1918, aimed at a "national system of public education available to all persons capable of profiting thereby." The Act laid stress on the need to provide further education for those who were unable to pay for it, but who "were capable of profiting thereby." The school leaving age was laid down at 14 years,

6

with powers by local authorities to raise it to 15. There is no record of any local authority imposing this extra year. The "half time" system, whereby a scholar could attend school for half a day, and work the other half day, was completely abolished. An Act of 1911 had abolished this system as far as industry was concerned, but it had continued in farming. Children under 12 years of age were forbidden entirely to work for gain, and the 12-14s were restricted to two hours a day. With many mothers helping the war effort, in munitions factories and other places, the need for nursery schools became more and more urgent. Fisher's Act gave local authorities power to establish and assist such schools for children from two to four years of age. Provision was made for 14-year-olds to continue their education at higher elementary schools and at Central schools. Increased grants were made available to Secondary Schools, and to provide State scholarships from Secondary Schools to the universities.

In their leisure hours boys were, on the whole, better catered for than girls. Among the uniformed boys' organisations was the Boys' Brigade, whose founder and secretary, Sir William Alexander Smith, died as recently as 10th May, 1914. He founded the Brigade in 1883, and lived to see the movement well established in Britain and overseas. With its drills and Bible Classes, and its emphasis on the cultivation of habits of obedience, reverence and discipline, the Brigade aimed to train boys to become God-fearing, self-reliant men. Every company of the Brigade was based upon a church, either Established or Free. In spite of the call-up denuding the movement of many of its officers the Boys' Brigade carried on during the war years, leading boys to "a true Christian manliness".

Since 1907, when General Sir Robert Baden-Powell held his historic camp for boys on Brownsea Island, the Boy Scout movement had made spectacular progress. On joining the movement a boy solemnly promised to do his duty to God and the King, to help other people at all times, and to obey the Scout laws.

All this, allied to a love of camping and the open air, and inspired by a spirit of adventure and service, were markedly appropriate to wartime. When war broke out Sir Robert approached Lord Kitchener with an offer to raise a corps of ex-Scouts or ex-South African Constabulary officers and men. Kitchener thanked the hero of Mafeking for his offer, but declined it. Sir Robert, Kitchener felt, would do more good by carrying on with his work as Scout leader.

During the war Boy Scouts did excellent service by acting as sentries to protect railway bridges, waterworks, telegraph and cable lines, and by acting as messengers. The work was handicapped by a shortage of Scoutmasters who were serving in the armed forces. Older men and women carried on the work in their absence. In towns and cities, churches and other philanthropic organisations had their non-uniformed organisations, their working lads clubs, and the like, providing recreation away from undesirable influences and company.

And what of the girls? There was the Girls' Friendly Society, founded in 1875, as a Church organisation to unite girls and women in a fellowship of prayer, service and purity of life. The Girls' Life Brigade, founded by the National Sunday School Union in 1902, aimed to provide girls with character and physical training and recreation. Like the Boys' Brigade it emphasised loyalty to the Church, and encouraged Bible study. First aid, home nursing, household management and child care were also taught. When the Boy Scout movement was launched many girls clamoured for a similar movement for their sex. Girl Scouts, as they called themselves at first, forced themselves upon Baden-Powell's notice when they appeared, complete with poles and knapsacks, at the Crystal Palace Boy Scout rally in 1909. Until 1915 the movement was a struggling one, although Baden-Powell had the help of his sister, Agnes, in organising the girls. Then, in 1915, Baden-Powell ensured the official recognition of the Girl Guides, as they were now called, by obtaining for them a Charter of Incorporation from the Board of

Trade. Baden-Powell's wife, Olave, then took the matter in hand, beginning with the scattered groups in Sussex, the county where the Baden-Powells lived. She enlisted the help various influential people could spare from their service to the war effort. She was so successful that in October, 1916, she was appointed Chief Commissioner for the Guides, and asked to do for other counties what she had been able to do for Sussex. In 1918 she became Chief Guide for the whole of the British Empire. By the end of the war the number of Guide Commissioners had risen from 160 in 1916 to 3,000. Olav's book, *Training Girls as Guides,* price 1/-, told everything a Guide Commissioner should know. Her husband's companion handbook, *Girl Guiding,* also appeared in 1918. The two books together covered most aspects of the guiding movement. Sir Robert and Lady Baden-Powell did all in their power to encourage the spread of both Scouting and Guiding overseas, in the Empire, and beyond. Chile, France, U.S.A. and the Scandinavian countries had adopted the movement even before the Great War. The Baden-Powells firmly believed that young people who had camped and worked together, sung, laughed, danced, played and prayed together would in later life be less likely to make war upon each other.

Evidence for the need of the activities of the voluntary work described above was not difficult to find in wartime Britain. When father was in the trenches, and mother was helping to keep him supplied with ammunition by going out to work, parental restraint fell to a dangerous level. Juvenile delinquency inevitably increased. So did the illegitimacy rate, which was by 1918 30 per cent above the 1914 figure. A notable piece of wartime child care was performed by the sisters Margaret and Rachel McMillan. In 1914 they founded the first open-air nursery school, at Deptford. They enlarged this, in response to wartime needs, as a crêche where the children of women munitions workers were cared for on payment of a modest fee of 7d. per day. Thus and thus the war years passed for British children, in all their countless intermediary stages between rags and riches, rickets and robust health, from elementary to public school education.

Chapter 10

FOOD AND DRINK

VICTORY in war depends, in part only, upon the courage and efficiency of the soldier at the fighting front. For the weapons of war the soldier depends upon the people at home. The morale of both soldier and civilian is another vital factor. Morale can only be sustained if there is a feeling that the war is a just one, is being properly conducted, and that there are adequate supplies of food and drink for all. Man certainly does not live by bread alone, but he cannot live without bread. As the weeks and months of war passed by the problem of obtaining sufficient food for the civilians loomed larger and larger.

As early as February, 1915, the German Government announced the intention of using her submarines to sink every merchant vessel in the seas around the British Isles. Alleging that British vessels sometimes flew the flags of neutral countries, the Germans warned that they could not therefore guarantee the safety of passengers and crews from neutral nations. Unable to force a decision on any of the fighting fronts, Germany would use the weapon of blockade, by mine and submarine, to bring down the obstinate British people. Since Britain depended, to a substantial and dangerous degree, upon her imports of food and raw materials, this weapon threatened the very prospect of an Allied victory. Germany stepped up her production of submarines, and the situation grew monthly more threatening for the food supplies of the British public. By the end of 1916 nearly one fifth of British tonnage in merchant vessels existing in August, 1914, no less than 2,300,000 tons had been sent to the bottom of the sea. The British public was feeling the impact of this un-British way of waging war. Encouraged and stimulated by the resounding and continuing success of their submarine campaign the German Government decided to throw off all restraints, and on 1st February, 1917, announced unrestricted submarine warfare. All shipping proceeding to, or from, Allied ports, would be sunk at sight, and without warning. By this means they hoped that before the year 1917 had passed a starving Britain would be suing for peace.

The Germans had a good basis for this hope of surrender through starvation. A new sight appeared increasingly in the streets of British towns and cities—queues, long queues of more or less patient people, waiting sometimes for hours for a pound or two of potatoes, or a few ounces of bacon. In March, 1917, when the people in one part of Cardiff heard that a certain shop had received a supply of potatoes for sale, they formed a queue, four deep, stretching for 600 yards, from 7 a.m. to 4 p.m. In April, 1917, some Londoners learned that at a farm in Farnborough, Kent, potatoes would be sold in shilling lots. They came in cars and buses, and made a queue, four deep, stretching for a mile. So great was the agitation at the prospect of possibly missing the shilling's worth of potatoes, that at one time the sale was suspended, while the police restored order. Margarine was another commodity in short supply, and much sought after. On a bleak December morning in 1917, a crowd of 3,000 assembled outside a shop in London's Walworth Road. Unhappily the supply of margarine was sufficient only for the first 2,000 in the queue, and the remaining 1,000 were sent empty away, after waiting vainly for two hours. Queues sometimes began to assemble at 5 o'clock on winter mornings.

The tedium of waiting was enlivened by retailing experiences in other queues, each teller adding a little. A member of a queue

in a northern industrial town heard stories of how, in one tussle
for food, a boy's ribs had been crushed in, in another a woman's
eye had been gouged out with a hat pin. In yet another queue
a woman was reported to have given birth to a child. Upon
investigation it was revealed that none of these stories were
actually based on fact, though it was true that a woman with
a baby in her arms had fainted after standing for two hours in
a queue for bacon.

Manual workers complained bitterly of having to subsist for
from eight to twelve hours of heavy process work on nothing
more substantial than bread and jam. Food supplied to troops
in training was not always either substantial or nourishing.
Private W. E. Sangster, later the Rev. Dr. Sangster, of Westminster Methodist Central Hall, later wrote of the appalling
meals served up in London to soldiers in training. Half raw and
sour sausage meat, bad potatoes and pallid, sodden "plum duff"
were some people's idea of "the stuff to give the troops". However, when Private Sangster was transferred to Norfolk, he
found a great improvement in the diet. In December, 1917, the
London *Times* listed sugar, tea, butter, margarine, lard, drip-
ping, milk, bacon, pork, condensed milk, rice, currants, raisins,
spirits and Australian wines, as all in short supply. Clearly, if
the morale of the nation was to be maintained, and the war
won, vigorous measures were needed to ensure that all were
adequately fed.

Action was taken against the submarine menace by the introduction of the convoy system, whereby ships sailed in groups
protected by naval vessels. This plan proved effective in reduc-
ing the number of sinkings by submarines, but a full description
of its workings has no place in this book. Nevertheless convoys
played a vital part in winning the war.

In view of the acute and widespread discontent the Government decided to ration food. As long ago as 1903 a Government appointed Royal Commission had examined the conditions of food supply and distribution in the event of a major

war. The Commission reported, in 1905, that there was rarely more than seven weeks supply of food in the country at any given time. In 1917 a Ministry of Food was established and rationing officially introduced. Sugar, butter, margarine, lard, meat, jam, cheese and tea, were all rationed. Everyone had a card containing coupons valid for a specific amount of each rationed food, and was required to register with a particular dealer. Unfortunately the Government neglected to stipulate fixed prices for the various commodities, which led to much profiteering. Bread was not rationed, but beans and other substances were mixed with the flour to make "war bread", which was darker in colour than the white to which the British public were accustomed. When tea (at 4/- per pound) was in short supply, the public was exhorted to buy loose cocoa, at 7½d. per quarter pound. If one found the meat ration inadequate there was always Symington's Soups, in thirteen varieties, described in the advertisements as "far more nourishing than meat," and providing enough soup for the whole family in one 2½d. or 4½d. packet. For breakfast "nourishing, satisfying oats, at 4d. per pound—5 breakfasts for 2d.," were available all through the war years. So was Nestle's Milk, "the richest in cream," at 1/1½d. per tin. Those who were doing well financially, out of the war, could buy herrings in tomato, crayfish, Black Leicester mushrooms, finest honey and apricots in syrup, and no coupons required, from Fortnum and Mason's.

To supplement his rations with wholesome, health giving vegetables and fruit, the citizen was recommended to take and cultivate an allotment garden. Thousands of men who hardly knew the difference between a gardening fork and a spade began to discover the joys and pains of work on the land. Those who had uncultivated back gardens were advised to dig them up, and to sow them with vegetables. Many thousands of additional acres were brought under cultivation as allotment gardens. The number of allotment holders increased from 600,000 in 1914 to 1,400,000 at the end of the war. In their efforts to feed the nation the farmers' depleted staffs of labourers were supplemented by 30,000 German prisoners of war. There were some anxious moments about the food supply in July, 1918, when heavy storms of rain damaged the crops. Fortunately August was a drier month, and the bulk of the harvest was secured. But September brought more rain, and in the Midlands and in Scotland much corn sprouted in the fields. In spite of these setbacks it was estimated that four-fifths of the 1918 harvest was reaped. The supply of agricultural land was further increased when Hampstead Heath and various parks up and down the country were ploughed up and planted with potatoes and other crops.

These strenuous measures proved effective. In spite of one compulsory meatless day per week when no meat, cooked or uncooked, could be sold, imposed in January, 1918, by the summer of that year meat, sugar, butter, margarine, lard, jam, marmalade and tea were all in regular, if small, supply to the whole population. The public was requested never to eat more than their share, and never to waste the least little bit. The genteel habit of leaving a little food on the side of the plate, "for Mr. Manners", was condemned for the duration of the war. The public was also requested not to keep hens, since hens required grain, and every cargo of grain sunk by enemy submarines had to be made up by economy in our homes.

Grain was not only useful to feed hens, and so produce eggs, it was also used, in vast quantities, to provide the British working man with his beer and whisky. This led to a situation in which Britain came near to wartime prohibition of intoxicating liquors. The Demon Drink came under fire, not only from the Temperance Movement, but also from any people who had never before associated themselves with this cause. In a letter to Prince Albert (later King George VI), in 1915, King George V wrote: "We must have more ammunition before we can try another advance. We can't turn it out fast enough. Drink, I am afraid, has something to do with it, so I have set the example by giving it up during the war." The wine cellars at Buckingham Palace were sealed for the duration. But, in spite of the eloquence of Lloyd George, Asquith and most other members of the Cabinet, refused to follow the King's lead. But the King and the members of the Royal Household continued to abstain, publicly and privately, until the war was over.

Lloyd George, in his journeying up and down Britain, thundered continuously against the menace of intemperance. "Drink is doing more damage in the war than all the German submarines put together," he told a Bangor audience in February, 1916. "We are fighting Germany, Austria and drink, and as far as I can see, the greatest of these three deadly foes is drink," he warned members of the Shipbuilders' Employers' Federation, in April, 1916. He toyed with the idea of buying out the drink industry, and nationalising it. But he was advised that this was beyond Britain's financial resources in time of war. Yet, however unpalatable the truth about alcohol drinking might be, as the war situation worsened, it became obvious that stricter controls must be introduced. If the consumer and the Trade could not control their propensities, then in the public interest the State must step in, as it had been doing for centuries past, and impose the necessary restraints. Absenteeism in industry was only one of the problems raised by the drinking habits of the British working man. Conan Doyle in a letter to *The Times,* complained of harpies in London who carried off lonely soldiers, made them drunk, and then infected them with venereal disease. The Temperance Council of the Christian Churches, which included Roman Catholics, Anglicans and Free Churchmen, was established in 1915: "to secure legislative and other reforms" in matters appertaining to the manufacture, supply and distribution of intoxicants. As early as November, 1914, the Vicar of Tamworth, Staffordshire, in his parish magazine, was complaining about the mistaken hospitality given by misguided, though well meaning, people, to troops billeted in that town.

"Some people think they cannot be kind or hospitable to their guests unless they give them alcohol," he wrote. "The Licensed

91

Victuallers here, with true public spirit, closed their houses early to men in uniform, but some people, especially women, hang about the billets; and press the soldiers to allow them to fetch them beer. We have heard of a case where guests invited out to tea had their tea doctored with whisky. There is no kindness in this. It only gets men into trouble."

In 1916 came the Report of the Royal Commission on Venereal Diseases, stating that there was "abundant evidence of an intimate connection between alcohol and venereal disease" and that "a decrease in the use of alcohol will be an important factor in diminishing the prevalence of venereal disease."

Arthur Mee, of *Children's Encyclopaedia* and *Children's Newspaper* fame, produced a very informative paperback entitled *The Fiddlers,* calling attention to the grave threat to the nation's food supplies, and asking: "How long will you (the people) go on fiddling? Till we starve?"

Mr. Mee pointed out that in the first thousand days of the war, from August, 1914 to May, 1917, no less than 4,400,000 tons of grain and 340,000 tons of sugar had been consumed in the manufacture of intoxicating liquors. On the basis of rations in April, 1917, this would have provided flour for the whole United Kingdom for 43 weeks, and sugar for the whole United Kingdom for 33 weeks. Sailors were losing their lives to bring food to our shores, and we were actually destroying food, since almost all the nourishing qualities of the grain was lost in the process of manufacture of the intoxicants. The temporary sense of euphoria experienced through drinking was hardly enough to justify this colossal waste. Mr. Mee indignantly wrote of a London wine and spirit firm that guaranteed delivery of its products right to the front line, though they had to limit their supply to officers, and to not more than 1 cwt. at a time.

A group of patriotic businessmen made an attempt to bring about prohibition of the manufacture and sale of all beers, wines and spirits for the rest of the war. The national press carried whole page advertisements setting out the case for personal abstinence and for nationwide prohibition. No less than 2,002,600 patriotic citizens signed an appeal to the Government to prohibit the traffic in intoxicants during the war and the period of demobilisation. 2,500 leaders in various circles of national life, scarcely any of whom had previously been connected with the cause of Temperance, identified themselves with the appeal. Britain came nearer to prohibition during those desperate months in 1917 than ever before, or since, in her history.

These proposals, of course, provoked strong opposition. One of the leading opponents of the proposals was that friend of the British working man, Mr. Horatio Bottomley. He saw in these drastic measures a denial of the freedom of the British working man to spend his hard-earned money as he pleased, to get drunk on Saturday night and then to beat up his long-suffering wife, rights exercised much more freely in pre-1914 days than in the more sober era that followed the First World War.

But, in spite of the eloquence of Mr. Lloyd George, the example of the King and the public opinion organised by the aforementioned businessmen, under the impressive title of the Strength of Britain Movement, the Government stood firm against the proposal of wartime prohibition.

In 1917 there was widespread discontent among munitions, land and other workers concerning the scarcity and high price of beer. Drinking was, after all, the simplest form of escaping for a while from the fears, anxieties and responsibilities of wartime. It filled a psychological need for a support, to "get away from it all" for a while. If the Government took away this support, what would the Government put in its place? The Government had nothing to offer the worker as a superior substitute, and without the anti-social side effects of intoxicants. To deprive the working man of his beer might cause such disruption as would lose Britain the war. So the Government decided to compromise. They decided against absolute prohibition, but introduced strict controls on the supply and sale of intoxicants. The

Central Control Board (Liquor Traffic), in 1916 appointed an Advisory Committee "to consider the conditions affecting the physiological action of alcohol, and more particularly the effects on health and industrial efficiency produced by the consumption of beverage of various alcoholic strengths." This committee included men like William McDougall, Reader in Mental Philosophy in the University of Oxford, F. W. Mott, Pathologist to the London County Asylums, and W. C. Sullivan Medical Superintendent of the Rampton State Asylum for Criminal Lunatics.

The Central Control Board, which ordered the investigation had Lord D'Abernon as its president, and included such diverse personalities as the Reverend Henry Carter, a Wesleyan minister, and Mr. W. Waters Butler, director of a Midland firm of brewers. In their Report the committee indicated that the British public spent more on alcoholic drinks than they did on meat, and more than twice what they spent on bread; that alcohol was a narcotic and not a stimulant; that its nutritional value was very small; that it contained no vitamins; that its alleged warming properties were illusory, and that it was in no way necessary for a healthy life. Furthermore, its misuse was a serious factor in crime, poverty, ill health and industrial inefficiency. Backed by this massive weight of incontrovertible evidence, the Government acted sharply and effectively. London pubs had been open for $19\frac{1}{2}$ hours daily, and provincial pubs for 18 hours. Opening hours were reduced to $5\frac{1}{2}$ per day, with an afternoon break, and to $4\frac{1}{2}$ hours on Sundays. The "Output of Beer Restriction Act" reduced production, by November 1918, to a mere 28 per cent of the 1914 amount. Spirits and beer were diluted, and the import of wines drastically reduced "Treating" was forbidden.

Although Mr. Lloyd George's suggestion for buying out the drink industry, and nationalising it, came to nothing, one small experiment in this direction was made at Carlisle. Here thousands of Irish labourers, on war work, were left with no better provision for spending their leisure hours, than the public houses. The results were very bad for the war effort, as well as for the men themselves. For £700,000 the Government bought up the breweries and the licensed premises in the area. Drunkenness was reduced, though the evidence suggests that this was due more to the restrictions on strength and supply, rather than to nationalisation of the traffic.

All these restrictions, accepted by the nation at large as a grim necessity, left a permanent legacy of good. The lighter ales and restriction on opening hours, together with counter-attractions to be described in the next chapter, all combined to break many a working man of his habit of getting drunk, or very fuddled every Saturday night, with the unpleasant and hurtful results to his wife and family.

So the British public tightened its collective belt, and came through the war years. In spite of such restrictions as bread not to be sold before it was twelve hours old, a ban on the manufacture for sale of light pastries, muffins, crumpets and tea cakes, and the drastic reductions described on the manufacture and sale of beer, wines and spirits, the British men, women and children ate and drank what they could obtain, and were as merry as the trying times allowed.

Chapter 11

ESCAPING FROM IT ALL

"O that I had the wings of a dove! For then I would fly away, and be at rest," sighed the troubled Psalmist three thousand or so years ago. In the wartime years millions of civilians echoed the Psalmist's longing to escape from the strains, tensions and anxieties of life. In their various ways most people contrived to find some temporary escape from their tribulations, and so to forget the war for a little time, at least. Some, we have already noticed, took the alcoholic escape route. The shortest way out of wartime Britain was through the public house! Alas! Those who tried to drown their troubles in drink merely found that they had taught them to swim! Others, as we have noted found a temporary escape in the pleasures of gardening, in getting back to nature, and at the same time "doing their bit" to win the war, by producing vegetables and fruit.

In the absence of radio and television to entertain people in their homes, theatres, music halls, cinemas and restaurants prospered exceedingly. In London, at the outbreak of war, plays being currently presented included J. M. Barrie's *The Little Minister,* at the Duke of York's Theatre, and Herbert Tree playing in *Drake,* at His Majesty's. For those with more frivolous tastes, Potash and Perlmutter headed the bill at the Queen's Theatre, and Albert Chevalier ("Knocked 'em in the Old Kent Road") and Billy Merson were entertaining at the Palladium

At the Palace Gaby Deslys starred in *The Passing Show*. In the provinces, at Birmingham, for instance, the citizens had the choice of stars like Gertie Gitana and Harry Weldon, or of being thrilled by the melodrama, *At the Mercy of the Mormons*. The music hall still flourished. George Robey, Harry Lauder, Marie Lloyd, Lupino Lane, Vesta Tilley and Florrie Forde were outstanding among those who were to provide music hall audiences with temporary distraction from the grimness of the times. The operas of Gilbert and Sullivan also enjoyed a wide popularity.

As 1914 gave way to 1915, and later years, an air of almost hysterical gaiety manifested itself in London. Soldiers on leave spent their money freely in theatres and restaurants and less desirable places. With grim realism, at the time of the massacres at Gallipoli and on the Western Front, the soldiers on leave told one another that money was no good to a corpse—which many of them would be within weeks. Bernard Shaw complained of the lack of demand for serious plays, a re-action from the grim realities of war. Life itself was quite serious enough, without spending precious time on leave pondering yet more human problems. In 1916, at the time of the blood bath on the Somme, the popular shows in London were : *A Little Bit of Fluff, Daddy Longlegs, Peg o' My Heart, Razzle Dazzle, The Bing Boys Are Here, The Bing Girls Are Here* and *Chu Chin Chow. The Maid of the Mountains* opened at Daly's Theatre on 10th February, 1917, and ran until 26th December, 1921, with José Collins in the leading role—no less than 1,352 performances. *Chu Chin Chow,* based on the story of *Ali Baba and the Forty Thieves,* with its lavish oriental setting and catchy tunes, with Oscar Ashe and Lily Brayton in the leading roles, opened at His Majesty's Theatre on 31st August, 1916, and continued until 22nd July, 1921, a total of 2,238 performances. The popular song writers admirably caught the mood of the times with *If you were the only girl in the world, and I was the only boy* and *There's a long, long trail awinding into the land of my dreams,* with their pronounced escape motif. *Pack up your troubles in your old*

97   7

kitbag, and smile, smile, smile and *Keep the home fires burnin*
had a patriotic appeal to maintain the war effort. *It's a long wa*
to Tipperary was a good marching song, written before the war
God save the King was first regularly played in theatres an
cinemas during the war years.

By 1914 the theatre and the music hall were beginning to fee
the impact of competition from a formidable alternative form
of popular entertainment—the cinema. In 1913 the first larg
studio specially designed for making films was built at Shepherd
Bush, by the Gaumont company. The war interrupted the mak
ing of films in Britain, and the Americans seized the opportunity
to develop films with a universal appeal. The British cinema
going public became familiar with names like Charlie Chaplin
Mary Pickford, W. S. Hart, Mabel Normand, Edna Purviance
Fatty Arbuckle, Bessie Love, Douglas Fairbanks, Pauline Fred
erick and Mae Murray. The American film director D. W
Griffith specialised in great spectacles and sweeping panoramas
His film *The Birth of a Nation,* with an American Civil Wa
setting, and *Intolerance* (depicting "Love's struggle through th
ages", and which stretched to three and a half hours of showing
time), were outstanding successes. Charlie Chaplin helped to
relieve a lot of wartime tension with his *Tillie's Puncture*
Romance, Shoulder Arms, and other comedies. Thriller serials
shown in two-reel instalments over fifteen or twenty weeks, wer
another popular feature of most cinema programmes. Million
were thrilled by the hairbreadth escapes of Pearl White in *Th*
Exploits of Elaine, The Perils of Pauline and *The House of Hate*
Five or six-reel versions of classical novels appeared on th
screens—*Tess of the D'Urbervilles, East Lynne, Edwin Drood*
among others. The cinema also entered the realm of teaching th
young, and preparing them for adult life. Mothers who hesitate
to acquaint their daughters with the facts of life were advised to
send them to see the film *Enlighten thy Daughter.* "It is no
longer necessary for mothers to teach their daughters," the ad
vertisement ran, "Just send them to the Picturedrome." By these

various means the cinema played its useful part in diverting the minds of the citizens from the grim realities of war for a little while. Not that the war was totally banned from the screen, for the short news reel formed a regular part of almost every cinema programme. *Pathé Gazette* and longer films like *War is Hell,* filmed at or near the fighting front, reminded cinemagoers of the inescapable realities of life in those days. The United States of America did not officially enter the war until 1917. But, through the medium of the cinema, and not least through the hilarities of custard pie throwing, and the thrills of the sheriff and his posse dealing with the Wild West rustlers, she made her contribution to maintaining the morale of the British people during those dark years. The older generation sometimes found difficulty in adjusting to the new form of entertainment. 66-year-old Robert Blatchford, the eminent Socialist journalist, and his wife, felt the need of a rest after a strenuous round of Christmas shopping in Regent Street, in December, 1917. They sought rest in what Mr. Blatchford described as "a kinema." "O, that kinema!" he afterwards wrote. To him, an intelligent member of the older generation, the entertainment was "a whirling, scurrying, unmeaning show . . . like a fevered and breathless nightmare. Squadrons of Mexicans and cowboys chased each other on wild horses over the wild prairie and wilder hills. Riders raced, guns fired, men fell, girls were abducted and rescued, a person in a slouch hat and decorated trousers, who might have been Ragtime Cowboy Joe, rode on horseback into a saloon, and wrecked the chandeliers and mirrors with his 'forty four', and when we came away was in the act of eloping with the general's daughter."

Prices of admission to these shows were generally low. In a typical northern industrial town the prices at one "bug house" cinema were as low as 1d., 2d. and 3d., and babies in arms were admitted free. A more usual range of prices was from 2d. up to 1/-.

For those who wished to "eat out" before, or after, a visit to the cinema, or theatre, prices remained reasonable. In April,

1916, the London Restaurant Wigmore advertised afternoon teas for 1/-, Table D'Hôte luncheons for 2/9d. and dinner for 4/6d. Ladies could still enjoy the delights of bargain hunting at Spring, Summer and Winter Sales. In January, 1918, Pontings, in Kensington High Street, advertised their Winter Sale. "Practical winter coats, in good quality velour blanket", were reduced from 3 guineas to 49/6d., together with many other startling reductions. There was, of course, a general increase in prices. In August, 1914, ladies could buy a crêpe de chine blouse for as little as $1/3\frac{1}{2}$d. By 1918 they were called upon to pay from 6/11d. for the same article. Throughout the war years there was never any real shortage of clothing or of many other goods. Ladies, therefore, could always find some temporary escape from the war in the pleasures of shopping.

For those who wished to escape from their dreary, smoky towns, into the pure air and beauty of the countryside, bicycles remained in good supply all through the war years. The motor car was still in its early days, and much of the energy of the industry was harnessed to the war effort. Nevertheless, early in 1915 a Morris Cowley car was produced, costing 158 guineas. It was powered by an American engine, and equipped with electric lighting. Previously Morris cars had relied on acetylene for the front lamps, and oil for the rear lamps. In that same year, 1915, a general order prohibited the import of motor parts, except for commercial purposes.

In those days before the British Broadcasting Corporation had introduced the millions to the delights of the symphony and the concerto, and while gramophone recording was of very poor quality, relatively few people could enjoy the pleasures of classical music. Sir Henry Wood contrived to maintain his promenade concerts at the Queen's Hall. The declaration of war brought many letters demanding the withdrawal of all German music, Wagner's in particular. After a while, when hysteria had subsided, German music was reinstated, even Wagner's. Recruiting thinned the ranks of both orchestra and promenaders. The 1914

Plate 9—Trainee bus conductorette on duty, September 1917. *(Photo: Hulton Picture Library.)*

Plate 10—Grocery store run entirely by women, August 1915.
(Photo: Hulton Picture Library.)

promenade concert season made a delayed start in mid-August, with a re-scored National Anthem and the *Marseillaise*. The menace of the Zeppelin combined with the dimmed streets to make the 1915 season almost a disaster. In desperation "Matinée Proms" were tried, and quickly abandoned, as only a few dozen people attended. However, in spite of depleted audiences and a depleted orchestra, Sir Henry carried on. In the event of a Zeppelin raid the audience receded under the balcony—in itself a sad commentary on the numbers present. Sir Henry received a tempting offer to cross the Atlantic, to take charge of the Boston Symphony Orchestra, but he decided that his place was in England. In spite of the demands of war new artists appeared, and helped to maintain the Proms. One of these was a child prodigy, the 11-year-old boy, Soloman, playing the solo part in Tchaikowsky's B flat minor piano concerto. The pianists Moiseiwitsch and William Murdoch, and the violinist, Albert Sammons, were among the new artists heard at Queen's Hall during those years. The new singers included Norman Allin and Frank Mullings. Concerts were sometimes unduly prolonged if the Zeppelins lingered long over London. The advertised programme performed, the audience, under the balcony, sang songs like *Tipperary*, and listened to an impromptu concert provided by orchestra and artistes, until the "All clear" was heard. Other orchestral conductors who enjoyed fame at that time included Sir Thomas Beecham, Sir Landon Ronald, Albert Coates, included Dame Clara Butt, Adelina Patti (who emerged from Hamilton Harty and Eugene Goossens. Great singers of the day retirement to sing for charity), Carrie Tubb and Gervase Elwes. Clara Butt, a devoutly religious woman, was particularly active in good works, organising many charity concerts at which she appeared. She organised a whole week of performances of Elgar's *Dream of Gerontius* in the Royal Albert Hall. "We are a nation in mourning," she said. "I want to give the people a week of beautiful thoughts, for I am convinced that no nation can be truly great that is not truly religious." Her concert in the Royal

101

Albert Hall, in aid of the work of the Red Cross, raised £9,000, Clara paying all the expenses. During this concert Clara sang *The Lost Chord, Land of Hope and Glory,* and *Abide With Me.* The concert concluded with Clara singing Costa's setting of *God Save the King,* backed by a choir 250 strong, and the massed bands of the Brigade of Guards. Among the audience were the King, the Queen and Princess Mary.

In the cottage and other homes of England, when the day's house or factory work was done, many thousands of women occupied some of their leisure hours in knitting for the troops. They produced socks, balaclava helmets, mittens, scarves and body belts to help to keep out the cold from the men in the trenches.

Or you could quietly read the daily paper or a popular weekly. The *Daily Mail, Daily Sketch, Daily Express, Daily News, Daily Chronicle* and *Daily Mirror* were all priced at ½d. when war began, though the price rose to 1d. before the Armistice. The "quality" newspapers, even *The Times,* cost only 1d. in 1914. Inevitably they devoted much space to news from the battle-fronts, but they found room for other horrors on the domestic front. There was, for instance, the infamous Smith and the Brides in the Bath case. George Joseph Smith, who was arrested on 1st February, 1915, was an ex-reformatory boy, with a criminal record going back to 1891. He was described as a "professional and literal ladykiller, of singular personality and charm over women." He regarded women purely as commercial propositions. The murders he committed followed the same pattern. He married the lady, made sure that she made a will in his favour, and then drowned her in her bath. The sensational trial of Smith opened on 22nd June, 1915, and lasted for nine days. Sir Edward Marshall Hall, thought by many to be the finest defence advocate of the day, was briefed for Smith. This was made possible by the Press providing the necessary funds if Smith, after his trial, would assign the copyright of anything he wrote to these newspapers. In spite of Sir Edward's eloquence he triple coincidence was too much for any jury to accept, and hey found Smith guilty. An appeal was rejected. Readers earned how, in the interval between sentence and execution, Smith's hair turned white, and how, though he called himself an atheist when he entered prison, he professed conversion to Christianity, and was confirmed by the Bishop of Croydon. His ast words were: "I am innocent." Marshall Hall, who was convinced that Smith was a hypnotist, also felt that the great care taken over the trial of this one man, at a time when thousands were daily being killed, was a great tribute to our judicial system. Another case which aroused profound interest was that of Lieut. Douglas Malcolm, who was found not guilty of either the murder or the manslaughter of Anton Baumberg, a Russian who made love to Mrs. Malcolm while her husband was away on active service.

Another home front horror that hit the headlines was what was described as "the blackest day in the history of British railways." On Whit Saturday, 22nd May, 1915, five trains were involved in a collision at Quintinshill, near Gretna Green. They comprised two troop trains, the midnight express from London (Euston) to Glasgow, a local train and a coal train. To add to the horror one troop train caught fire from escaping gas from the cylinders. In all the dead numbered 226, the majority of them soldiers on their way to Gallipoli. One of the troop trains, measuring 213 yards long, was telescoped to 67 yards by the violence of the impact. Two signalmen were arrested and convicted of manslaughter.

The newspaper read, the citizen could then turn to one or other of a variety of popular weeklies like *Answers, Titbits, Penny Pictorial, Pearson's Weekly, Women's World* or *Peg's Paper.* The more religiously minded had their *Christian Herald, Sunday Companion, Methodist Recorder, Church Times* or *British Weekly.* Boys and girls, too old for the "comics" mentioned in a previous chapter, had the *Magnet, Gem* and *Penny Popular,* featuring the boys of Greyfriars, St. Jim's and Rookwood schools, the *Marvel, Sexton Blake Library* and *Boys' Own Paper*. In spite of paper shortages, resulting in reduction of size, all these and many other periodicals continued to appear throughout the war years, to divert the minds of the masses from their trials and troubles for a while.

Some of the established novel writers continued to produce their fictional works, but others like Arnold Bennett and John Galsworthy, produced nothing in the way of full length stories. H. G. Wells' wartime novels included *Bealby* (1915), *Mr. Britling Sees it Through* (1916), and *Joan and Peter* and *The Soul of a Bishop* (1918). To help his fellowmen to understand the times they were living in he wrote *The War and Socialism* (1915), *What is Coming?* (1916), *The Elements of Reconstruction* (1916), *War and the Future* and *God the Invisible King* (1917) and *In the Fourth Year* (1918). Conan Doyle abandoned Sherlock Holmes and devoted his energies to writing six serial volumes of *A History of the British Campaigns in France and Flanders.* John Buchan produced two best-selling thrillers, *The Thirty Nine Steps* and *Greenmantle.* The year 1915 saw Virginia Woolf's first novel, *The Voyage Out,* and Compton Mackenzie's *Guy and Pauline,* a story full of warmth and sunshine. Greatest of all the wartime novels, perhaps, was Somerset Maughan's *Of Human Bondage* (1916). Other novels worthy of a mention were Clemance Dane's *Regiment of Women,* George Moore's *The Brook Kerith* and D. H. Lawrence's *The Rainbow.* Thomas Hardy, Marie Corelli and Hall Caine (the uncrowned king of the Isle of Man), remained silent in their retirement from the world of books. Havelock Ellis went on writing his voluminous *Studies in the Psychology of Sex,* which occupied him from 1897 to 1928. Quiller Couch published his *On the Art of Writing* in 1916, and in the last year of the war Lytton Strachey's lively and impudent challenge to conventional content, *Eminent Victorians,* made its appearance.

In spite of the great demand for light and frivolous entertainment, some playrights still produced more serious work. On the eve of the war Bernard Shaw finished *Heartbreak House,* portraying the cultural, leisured pre-war Europe, idle, hypochondriacal and shallow. The play was not produced until after the war, during which time Shaw began his *Back to Methusalah.* John Masefield's *Good Friday* and John Drinkwater's *Abraham Lincoln* were two other serious wartime plays. J. M. Barrie's wartime efforts included four war playlets, *The Old Lady Shows Her Medals, The New Word, Barbara's Wedding* and *A Well Remembered Voice,* in addition to *A Kiss For Cinderella* and *Dear Brutus.* On the lighter side, too, was Harold Brighouse's *Hobson's Choice.*

The poets found much to inspire—or provoke—them in those stirring times. The Poet Laureate, appointed in 1913, was Robert Bridges. His anthology, *The Spirit of Man,* was published in January, 1916. Rudyard Kipling, whom some said should have been Poet Laureate in preference to Bridges, wrote *For All We Have and Are* in the early months of the war. He warned that "The Hun is at the gate," and boldly asked:

> What stands if freedom falls?
> Who dies if England live?"

Later came his poem *Minesweepers,* with its resounding refrain:

"Send up Unity, Claribel, Assyrian, Stormcock and Golden Grain."

Thomas Hardy, silent in the matter of novels, came up in the first weeks of the war with his *Men Who March Away.*

War was still an accepted institution in 1914. The mood of the early months was captured in the poems of Rupert Brooke. War was thought of as a great cleansing and purifying agent in a world soiled by materialistic values. So Rupert Brooke could write of his generation as "swimmers into cleanness leaping." That was before the days of Passchendaele and Flanders mud.

Brooke died in hospital, at Scyros, on St. George's Day, 1915, still in the mood of his poem, *Now God Be Thanked, Who Has Matched Us For This Hour*. Julian Grenfell, who died of wounds at Boulogne, on 26th May, 1915, will always be remembered for his lines entitled *Into Battle*. Had these young poets, of such great promise, lived longer they might well have changed their tune, as did Siegfried Sassoon.

Later he was to write of war as "a bloody thing, half the youth of Europe blown through pain into nothingness." Another wartime poet was Lawrence Binyon, whose lines *For the Fallen* (They shall grow not old . . .") are often recited in Remembrance Day services.

Thus and thus, according to their tastes and temperaments, highbrow or lowbrow, at home or in places of public entertainment, the civilian population of wartime Britain found the necessary relaxation and respite which enabled them to carry on until an armistice was declared.

Chapter 12

THE MEN AT THE TOP

WHEN war broke out His Majesty King George V was 49 years of age, and in the fifth year of his reign. Born and brought up in the Victorian age, he was well endowed with the Victorian quality of moral earnestness. Father of five sons and a daughter, in family life he was a disciplinarian. On the wall of his library at Buckingham Palace hung the maxims:

"Teach me to be obedient to the rules of the game.
Teach me neither to proffer, nor to receive, cheap praise.
Teach me neither to cry for the moon, nor over spilt milk."

He read a chapter of the Bible every day. A good and sincere man, he was never a mere figurehead. As the years went by he emerged more and more as the father of his people, both in Britain and in her farflung Empire.

When war was declared one of his first actions was to offer the carriage horses from the Royal Stables for ambulance work, and the royal carriages to convey wounded men from the railway stations. His offer of Buckingham Palace as a hospital was respectfully declined. The Palace had never been designed with any such purpose in view, and was quite unsuitable. But his offer to place the Buckingham Palace gardens at the disposal of wounded officers was gratefully accepted. Throughout the war one constant aim of the King and the Queen was to get among the people over whom they reigned. The King undertook a number of tours of the munitions, engineering and shipbuilding establishments, upon which the soldiers at the Front depended for the means to beat the enemy. One extended tour embraced Merseyside and Manchester, Barrow-in-Furness, Workington and Gretna. Munitions factories and shipyards in these places were visited after a dangerous series of strikes had threatened the continuance of the war effort. Another tour took him to the shipbuilding and marine engineering works on Tyneside, Tees-side and Humberside. On another occasion he spent five days on Clydeside. All this was at a time when the yards were working all out to make good the losses of shipping sustained during the submarine campaign. In many places Arthur Henderson, Lloyd George's adviser in labour matters, arranged for His Majesty to meet leading Trade Unionists. By such means the King made his own unique and substantial contribution to maintaining vital production.

Visitation of hospitals, both in Britain and in France, was another regular part of the King's itinerary. Where there was sorrow, the King was there, as for instance, his visitation of the bereaved and homeless after the Silvertown explosion. Though this book is concerned only with life in Britain, reference must be made to the King's visits to the troops in France. Though he was never wounded by enemy action, his services to the troops involved him in a serious accident. His horse reared, while he was inspecting soldiers, fell on him and fractured his pelvis. Though he lived for nineteen years after this painful accident he was never, physically, the same man again.

In all his wartime services the King had the wholehearted support of his Queen. She, too, was tireless in visiting hospitals, at home and abroad. Immediately war was declared she lent her name to the workshops established to give work to unemployed women. Queen Mary's Workshops provided needed stopgap relief until the early months of 1915, when the massive

Plate 11—Chief officer and members of Ladies Fire Brigade, March 1916.
(*Photo: Hulton Picture Library.*)

Plate 12—King George V and Queen Mary visiting a boot repairing factory in the Old Kent Road, London. (*Photo: Imperial War Museum.*)

recruitment of women for war work rendered them unnecessary. When their Majesties felt the need, from time to time, to "get away from it all", they retired for short periods to York Cottage, Sandringham. Windsor Castle was too close to London for this purpose, and Balmoral Castle was closed for the duration.

As anti-German feeling grew the King himself was not exempt from criticism for his German connections. By a Proclamation dated 17th July, 1917, the King relinquished all his German titles and dignities. Further, as a member of the House of Saxe-Coburg-Gotha, he declared that all male descendents of Queen Victoria, who were also British subjects, should adopt the sur-name of Windsor. A happier occasion was their Majesties' Silver Wedding anniversary on 6th July, 1918. They drove, through cheering crowds, to a Thanksgiving Service at St. Paul's Cathe-dral, and afterwards to a presentation at the Guildhall. Their marriage was a truly happy one, and when their duties parted them from time to time, they maintained a daily correspondance.

Their oldest son, the handsome and charming Prince of Wales, the future Edward VIII, was twenty years old in 1914. He showed his mettle in being commissioned to the Grenadier Guards only two days after war was declared. In November, 1914, he sailed to France, as aide-de-camp to the Commander-in-Chief, Sir John French. He had a strong desire to be with the troops in the front line, but Authority refused to allow him to take the risk. Lord Kitchener explained to him that the danger to his life was only one risk. In the event of his death the Prince had brothers to succeed him. But there was another grave risk —that he should be captured and held as a prisoner of war by the Germans. That risk Authority resolutely refused to take. Nevertheless the Prince contrived to be under fire on the Western Front, from time to time. 1916 found him serving in Egypt, 1917 in Italy, and in 1918 he was back again in France.

Albert, Duke of York, the future George VI, 18 years of age when the conflict began, served in the Royal Navy. At that time he was a midshipman, aboard H.M.S. *Collingwood,* cruising in the Mediterranean.

Ill health plagued him for most of the war years. Temporary relief came when he was operated upon for appendicitis, at Aberdeen, in September, 1914. By the time of the Battle of Jutland, in 1916, he was a sub-lieutenant. He was present, and under fire, at this, the greatest naval battle of the war. In December, 1916, he was created a Knight of the Garter, and in the following May, appointed to H.M.S. *Malaga*. A few months later his health broke down completely, and a duodenal ulcer was diagnosed. A successful operation followed, and the Prince's health so improved that he was first appointed to the Royal Naval Air Service, and afterwards gazetted captain in the newly established Royal Air Force.

Princess Mary was also eager to make her contribution to the war effort. Seventeen years old when the war began, she trained as a nurse at the Great Ormond Street Hospital for children.

The war brought about the eclipse of the Royal Houses of Hohenzollern, Hapsburg and Romanov. But the House of Windsor emerged from the fiery trial stronger than ever in the affection and respect of the British people.

In the early days of the war the man who overshadowed everyone else in the public view was Herbert Horatio, First Earl Kitchener of Khartoum and of Broome. Asquith at once appointed him Minister of State for War. King George would have welcomed his appointment as Commander-in-Chief, with military authority over Sir John French. Sixty-four years of age, a lifelong bachelor, and an individualist of drive and determination, Kitchener was responsible for recruiting, the production of munitions, and for strategy. It was an impossible burden even for a man twenty years younger than Kitchener. Nevertheless he addressed himself to his Herculean task with great energy and enthusiasm. He was among the first to realise something of the magnitude of the war, and the stupidity of the shallow "all over by Christmas" attitude. At once he took steps to raise a large army of 70 divisions. He saw his "first 100,000" grow to

110

3,000,000, the largest volunteer force ever raised. Kitchener was never enthusiastic about conscription. He did not live to see that great army partially broken on the Somme. No one could have attracted recruits in such large numbers as he did, with his personality, his figure and his reputation for victory in the Sudan and in South Africa. The Government had been caught unprepared for war. Kitchener did more than anyone, in those early days, to retrieve the situation. In the matter of strategy, he foresaw the direction of the German attack in the direction of Mons, rather than from the Ardennes, as Joffre thought. He never entertained the possibility of the defeat of the British Empire, but he believed that Germany was too powerful to be beaten without aid from America.

On the debit side he undervalued the potential of the Territorial force, and more tragically still, he underestimated the importance of machine guns, high explosive shells and heavy guns in trench warfare. This led to widespread and hostile criticism. THE SHELLS SCANDAL. LORD KITCHENER'S TRAGIC BLUNDER ran the *Daily Mail* headlines. In spite of the fact that Kitchener's supporters publicly burned the *Daily Mail* on the Stock Exchange, action was taken to relieve Kitchener of some of his responsibilities. A separate Ministry of Munitions was established, with Lloyd George at its head, to speed the production of shells. That was in May, 1915, and in December of that year Kitchener's powers were further limited when Sir William Robertson was appointed Chief of the Imperial General Staff, with authority over Kitchener. The end of Kitchener's wartime service, and life, came with dramatic suddenness in June, 1916. At the invitation of Czar Nicholas II Kitchener departed for Archangel on a special mission to Russia, to investigate the state of affairs in that unhappy country, and how Britain might help. Kitchener sailed from Scapa Flow, aboard the cruiser *Hampshire*. Heavy seas caused the two escorting destroyers to return to port. The *Hampshire* struck a mine, and sank within fifteen minutes. All but twelve of those aboard were drowned,

111

Kitchener among the lost. The impact of this tragic news upon the British public was greater than that of the news of the German advance on Paris in 1918. Violet Bonham Carter, Asquith's daughter, compared it to the sudden fall of Nelson's Column, in Trafalgar Square, if that notable monument were suddenly to collapse at the feet of the public. In spite of intrigues against him, in spite of his being partially to blame for the failure of the Dardenelles expedition, and for his mishandling of the munitions situation, he was popular with the public to the end. Some found it too much to believe that he was really dead. He was not drowned, but engaged on a mission so secret that its nature, and his continued existence, could not be disclosed until the war was over! His death left a vacancy at the War Ministry. Lloyd George, having made a resounding success of the Ministry of Munitions, left that office and took over Kitchener's post. Lord Northcliffe, proprietor of the *Daily Mail,* and no friend of Kitchener's, very unkindly commented: "Providence is on the side of the British Empire after all!" But in spite of his human shortcomings, Kitchener was a great personality, and he materially influenced the course of the war in the Allies' favour.

An intellectual giant, a Fellow of Balliol College, a man in whom a fine intellect was allied to sound judgment and integrity of character, a man of courage, composure and great dignity. Such was the character of Britain's 62-year-old Prime Minister, Herbert Henry Asquith, in the fateful year 1914. His judgment on questions brought before him was invariably sound, and his presentation of those questions to Parliament was equally sound and convincing. According to Lord Morley, Asquith had missed his vocation. "He should have been a judge," the noble lord declared. There was much truth in this shrewd observation, for Asquith inclined to deal with questions, not when they arose, but when they were put before him. When Lloyd George said what a nice fellow Asquith was, Arthur Ackland replied: "Yes, but did you ever hear him make a suggestion of his own?" "Unshakable as a rock, and like a rock, incapable of movement," was historian A. J. P. Taylor's verdict on Asquith. A more devastating criticism ran : "For twenty years he has held a season ticket on the line of least resistance, and has gone wherever the train of events carried him, vividly justifying his position at whatever point he happened to find himself."

Many thought him somewhat out of touch with harsh conditions under which the working classes lived. But it was he, when he was Chancellor of the Exchequer, from 1906 to 1908, who laid the foundations of the old age pensions scheme, which his successor in office, Lloyd George, made a reality. When the hurricane burst upon the world in 1914 Asquith was well fitted to give dignified, if not rousing and vigorous, leadership to the British nation and Empire. An extract from one of his best remembered speeches, that made at the Mansion House, in November, 1914, ran : "We shall never sheathe the sword, which we have not lightly drawn, until Belgium has recovered all or more than she has lost."

1914 faded into 1915, and a great storm of criticism arose concerning the conduct of the war, in particular of the shortage of high explosive shells. As we have noted, Lord Kitchener bore the brunt of the acrimony, but Prime Minister Asquith was also blamed. Phrases he had used in the House of Lords controversy in 1911 were remembered, and used against him. "Wait and see! All will be well!," he assured the House of Commons at that time. The words were taken out of their context, and used to accuse him of dilatoriness in the time of Britain's peril. Dissension arose within the Cabinet. The Conservatives called for Coalition Government. Asquith retained his position as Prime Minister, and brought in Conservatives, notably Bonar Law as Colonial Secretary. But dissatisfaction with Asquith's alleged "Wait and see" policy was not allayed, and the demand for a more vigorous leadership steadily grew. Asquith's view was that politicians should keep out of the war while free enterprise made the weapons of war, for the generals to use to win battles. This view was not shared by Lloyd George and other

113

8

Cabinet colleagues. They agreed with the French statesman Briand, that "war is too serious a thing to be left to the soldiers.' On 4th December, 1916, this news item appeared in the papers :

"The Prime Minister, with a view to the more active prosecution of the war, has decided to advise His Majesty the King to consent to the reconstruction of the Government."

In this reconstructed Government Lloyd George became the Prime Minister. One who regretted the fall of Asquith was King George. Asquith himself remained outwardly calm and unshaken, but inwardly he was deeply wounded. He was always inwardly disturbed by malice, pettiness, intrigue and talebearing, but he was never known to retaliate in kind. At this time, too, he was grieving deeply following the death of his brilliant son, Raymond, who was killed in action, near Ginchy, while leading his men of the Grenadier Guards. A fair summing up of Asquith suggests that his many fine qualities made him a more successful peacetime, rather than wartime, Prime Minister. After the retirement of Campbell-Bannerman, in April, 1908, Asquith was Prime Minister continuously through eight and a half increasingly anxious and troubled years. The time then came for him to make way for a man who was second only to Kitchener in his appeal to the imagination and will-to-win spirit of the British people—David Lloyd George.

While Asquith was associated, in the minds of the people, with the upper classes, Lloyd George was undoubtedly a man of the people, who had known poverty and hardship. He was also known as a defender of the rights of the ordinary man and woman, his first widely publicised exploit being his successful action to establish the right of a Nonconformist to be buried in an Anglican churchyard.

Later came his provision for old age pensions, his scheme to "soak the rich", his National Insurance Act, and his association with the restricting of the powers of the House of Lords

He was known, too, as a man of peace. His opposition to the Boer War placed his life in danger, and made him, for a while, the most unpopular man in the country. In the last hectic week in July, 1914, he was the leader of the peace party in the Cabinet, hoping and striving to keep Britain out of a continental war. But when Belgium was invaded he threw himself wholeheartedly into the war effort. Since 1908 he had been Chancellor of the Exchequer, and he remained in this office until the great shell shortage scandal rocked the Government in 1915. As the first Minister of Munitions, in the newly formed Ministry, his energy and enthusiasm, and his skill in settling industrial disputes, did much to save the country from disaster on the battle fronts. After Lord Kitchener's untimely end he left the Ministry of Munitions to take over Kitchener's job as Secretary of State for War. Six months later, as we have noted, the growing public dissatisfaction with the Asquith regime, coupled with a demand for a more energetic and inspired leadership, resulted in Lloyd George becoming Prime Minister. In the early months of his Premiership, the first half of 1917, Britain was in danger of being starved into surrender by the success of the German submarine campaign. The problem was solved, as H. A. L. Fisher wrote, partly by the adoption, "forced on the Admiralty by Mr. Lloyd George, of the convoy system." In his thinking about the over-all strategy of the war Lloyd George was an "easterner". As the German lines in the west were almost impregnable, the attacking force must always suffer heavily. Therefore the Allies should remain on the defensive in the west, and concentrate on rallying the Balkan powers to attack the Austrian Empire, and upon establishing a safe channel for the munitioning of Russia. But the generals, both French and British, disagreed with this strategly. They pinned their faith to a great breakthrough in the west, thrust home by a spectacular cavalry charge. Lloyd George was strongly against the battle of Passchendaele, that tragic waste of British lives, when thousands of wounded drowned in the mud and water, the Germans yielding little ground, at the cost of

300,000 British casualties. Lloyd George questioned whether the French, their armies weakened by mutiny, could only be saved from destruction at such a cost. Britain, he felt, should have husbanded her manpower until the following year, until the Americans had arrived in France in force. However, on this occasion, the will of the generals prevailed, and thousands of British households were flung into what Lloyd George and others felt, as needless mourning.

Lloyd George, with his thickset figure, his piercing eye and persuasive tongue, his leonine head, remained in the office of Prime Minister for the rest of the war, until victory came, and he addressed himself to other aims like "homes for heroes" and to making Germany pay the cost of the war. But those matters lie outside the scope of this book. The Welsh Wizard, as he was called, deservedly finished the war very high in the esteem and affection of the British public. In the hour of need he had not failed them. He had given just that energetic and inspired leadership needed in those dark days. His speeches had enheartened and encouraged the nation as no other speaker's had. Yet, despite his shrewdness, his vision, his energy and persuasiveness, one who knew him observed that there was one feeling he did not inspire in those close to him—trust.

From the great First World War leader we turn to the man who was destined to become the great Second World War leader—Winston Spencer Churchill. He was 39 years of age when war began, and he occupied the office of First Lord of the Admiralty. He it was who so wisely kept together the British fleet after the July, 1914, manoeuvres were finished, and sent it to take up war stations at Scapa Flow and Rosyth. In his strategic thinking he was, like Lloyd George, an "easterner". He was one of the few who saw the possibilities of an armoured car on caterpillar wheels, which could push through barbed wire, trenches and other impediments, as the weapon to break the deadlock on the Western Front. Opponents of this revolutionary idea referred to the tank, as it came to be called, as "Winston's

Folly". Under Winston's vigorous leadership all German warships were swept from the high seas in the first four months of
the war. When Prince Louis of Battenburg relinquished his position as First Sea Lord, under pressure of anti-German feeling,
his place was taken by Lord John Fisher, who had served in the
navy since the days of the Crimean War. As First Sea Lord from
1904-10 he introduced the dreadnought and sponsored the
development of oil fuel and submarines in the Royal Navy. He
was then, in 1914, 73 years of age, and described as one who
"lived by instincts, hunches, flashes he was unable to justify or
sustain in argument." As might be expected, he and Winston
were uncomfortable colleagues, not helped by the fact that he
was no match for Winston in an argument. Fisher was strongly
opposed to the Gallipoli campaign, by which Winston hoped to
open a way to help Russia to maintain her war effort. If the
Navy could force a way through the Dardenelles, Russia might
have been provided with the necessary arms to keep her in the
war. Soon after the attack was launched Fisher resigned, declar-
ing that the ships required by the Grand Fleet in the North Sea
were being endangered. A few months later, the Dardenelles
campaign having failed, Winston was in disgrace, being un-
justly blamed for the defeat. An interim report from the Dardenelles Commission vindicated him, but in the minds of the
public it was long before he lived down the allegations about
his ill-fated "eastern" ideas to shorten the war. As he thought
of the new armies and the deadlock of the Western Front he felt
there was a greater chance of victory in the east, rather than in
the soldiers being sent to "chew barbed wire" in France.

The withdrawal of our forces from Gallipoli was followed by
Winston's relegation to the Duchy of Lancaster. This was a post
reserved for beginners in the Cabinet, or for politicians in the
first stages of decrepitude. Other men's fatal delays and mis-
handlings of the Gallipoli campaign rebounded on Winston,
who wrote of the way the campaign was conducted : "We have
sent two-thirds of what was necessary a month too late."[1]

Winston spent the months from November, 1915 to May, 1916 on active service on the Western Front, as Colonel of the 6th Royal Scots Fusiliers. He spent much of his time in the front line, and on one occasion, at least, narrowly escaped death. When his regiment was fused with another he lost his job, and returned to Parliament. When Lloyd George became Prime Minister, against strong opposition from Bonar Law and other Tories, he appointed Winston to the Ministry of Munitions. Winston threw himself into his work with characteristic energy and enthusiasm, fully justifying Lloyd George's faith in him. In his first six months at the Ministry the strength of the Tank Corps (his special concern), increased by 27 per cent. It was during his period at the Duchy of Lancaster that Winston found solace in painting. He felt his tensions released, and his frustrations evaporate, as he sat at his easel and set down the scene before him in vivid colours. His gift of painting word pictures was also in evidence, for instance in what Lloyd George called Winston's "morbid detestation" of the Russian Revolution. Talking of Czarist Russia and her collapse, Winston said : "With victory in her grasp, she fell upon the earth, devoured alive, like Herod of old, by worms." Changing the figure of speech, Winston described the Russian catastrophe thus : "The ship sank in sight of port. She had weathered the storm, but a feeble and foolish captain and a crew many of whom were on the brink of mutiny, her engines neglected and out of repair, caused her to founder." Thus Winston, an artist in words as well as paints, an organiser, a fighter, a man of vision and an individualist, made his unique and substantial contribution to the winning of the war.

Wars are fought in the realm of ideas, as well as on the battle-fields. What goes on in a man's mind vitally affects what he does with his hands. To maintain good morale, in both civilians and soldiers is a vital necessity if the war effort is not to collapse. To undermine the enemy's morale can mean his collapse. Hence the importance of propaganda. By the end of the war Britain's propaganda machine was in the hands of four capable men, three of them well known in the newspaper world. Minister of Information,

118

n 1918, was William Maxwell Aitken, better known as Lord
Beaverbrook. He was the son of a Canadian Presbyterian minister.
Born in New Brunswick, in 1879, he made a fortune in business
n Canada before coming to England in the early years of the
20th century. From 1910-16 he was Liberal Member of Parliament for Ashton-under-Lyne. After the fall of Asquith he was
bitterly disappointed when the Presidency of the Board of Trade,
promised to him by Lloyd George, went to Albert Stanley. At
the end of 1916 he bought, for £17,500, a controlling interest
n the *Daily Express,* with the idea of propagating his strong
views on the role and importance of the British Empire. 1918
found him, not only Minister of Information, but also Chancellor
of the Duchy of Lancaster. Beaverbrook never forgot that he
was a son of the manse. The influence of his early days lasted on
all through his life. The strength of his character was mingled
with gentleness. He could be gentle with the weak and vulnerable,
but tough with the strong. To a beginner in journalism he would
say: "Yes, you did that very well indeed, but let me make a
suggestion. . . ." He kept the *Daily Express* a family newspaper,
and steadfastly refused to rake the muck-heaps. It was also said
of him that he was "a goad and gold man." He put a goad in
men's pants, and gold into their pockets!

In his propaganda work he had the assistance of Albert Charles
William Harmsworth, better known as Lord Northcliffe, son of
a barrister-at-law, born at Dublin, in 1865. Northcliffe, during
the war years, was proprietor of the London *Times* as well as of
the first ½d. morning newspaper, the *Daily Mail,* which he
founded in 1896. He was appointed to serve with Beaverbrook
as Director of Propaganda in enemy countries. He and Beaverbrook collaborated in a series of very effective propaganda leaf-
ets. These could in no sense be described as 'lying propaganda'.
On the contrary they told the enemy the deadly truth about his
position and grim prospects. The guiding principle was to dis-
eminate among enemy soldiers and civilians those unpleasant
facts of which the German Government was very much aware,

and did not wish the people to know. The leaflet set out such truths as the menace of the growing number of American troops in France, and the failure of the German submarine campaign with details of the number of submarines which failed to return to their base. The leaflets were attached to small balloons, and were released whenever a strong west wind was blowing. They drifted into Belgium, into occupied France and into Germany itself.

In the later stages of the war Northcliffe's brother, Lord Rothermere undertook responsibility for propaganda to neutral countries. In 1914 he had acquired a controlling interest in the *Daily Mirror,* and in 1915 founded the *Sunday Pictorial.* As Air Minister he took a leading part in the amalgamation of the Royal Flying Corps and the Royal Naval Air Service as the Royal Air Force. Propaganda on the home front, and in the colonies, was in the hands of Rudyard Kipling, whose only son, John, an officer in the Irish Guards, was killed at Loos, in 1915.

Leader of the Opposition in the House of Commons, when war began, was Mr. Andrew Bonar Law. Like Lord Beaverbrook he was a son of the manse, a Canadian, born in New Brunswick, and son of a Presbyterian minister. Coming to England, as a successful businessman, he represented Bootle in the House of Commons, in the Conservative interest, from 1910-18. As has already been pointed out, he became colonial secretary in the first Coalition Government in 1915. When Asquith resigned, and Lloyd George became Prime Minister, Bonar Law became Chancellor of the Exchequer. It was a position he was well qualified to fill, for in the world of business he was outstanding for his remarkable grasp of the details of finance and of statistics. His position as Chancellor carried with it a seat in the war cabinet. His quiet and unthrusting disposition precluded him from ever becoming a great popular hero. But his shrewdness combined with his innate honesty gained him the respect, if not the adulation, of those who knew him. Of Lloyd George he said : "He is a very nice man. But he is the most dangerous man who ever lived."

One of the most unpopular, and misunderstood, men in Britain was James Ramsay MacDonald, the man who rose from the humblest beginnings to become the chief founder and first leader of the Labour Party, who survived a storm of detraction and abuse, and eventually became Prime Minister, not once, but three times. He was denounced as a pacifist—which he never was. He was also, on equally shaky evidence, denounced as a pro-German, and an arch-traitor. The day after war was declared he resigned the chairmanship of the Labour Party, and Arthur Henderson took his place. In December, 1914, he crossed to Belgium as a volunteer member of an ambulance unit organised by Dr. Hector Munro (the writer whose pseudonym was 'Saki'), and attached to the Belgian Army. He was at once summoned back to England. Lord Kitchener was annoyed at this, and gave MacDonald an omnibus pass to the Western Front as an official visitor. Armed with this MacDonald made extensive tours of the battle fronts, visiting Ypres and St. Omer, among other places, and from time to time came under enemy fire. Though he resigned the chairmanship of the Labour Party, he retained the position of Party treasurer throughout the war, and represented Leicester in the House of Commons. There he opposed conscription as unnecessary to win the war, as temptingly useful to industrial magnates and as a victory for militarism. He spoke at meetings called by the National Council for Civil Liberties, an all-party organisation. There he maintained the right of free speech, and advocated the reform or repeal of the Military Service Act. He looked with favour upon Kerensky's bloodless Russian revolution, in March, 1917, but not upon Lenin's take-over in November of that year.

The result of all this was that he was alleged to be in the pay of the Germans. He was therefore expelled from the Moray Golf Club, at Lossiemouth, by 73 votes to 24 votes. Many public halls in London and the provinces were closed against him, and many editors regretted that they could not publish the articles he submitted to them. Most people thought he deserved all this, and more, because he was "against the war." However, he was not entirely without friends, not least among his fellow countrymen. This was markedly apparent at the so-called "Battle of Plumstead Common", at an open air meeting he addressed on 31st August, 1918. A hostile crowd gathered, some of them armed with sticks spiked with nails. Wagonettes laden with empty beer bottles, missiles for throwing at the speaker, were observed in the vicinity. Fortunately for MacDonald, a body of kilted Highlanders arrived at Victoria Station that morning. Hearing that MacDonald was in danger, they sacrificed a precious day's leave, to ensure that he was not lynched by the angry mob. In spite of stones and beer bottles flying around his head MacDonald managed to make himself heard. His enthusiastic bodyguard then escorted him several hundred yards to the waiting taxi, and to safety.

The clue to the understanding of MacDonald's behaviour during the war is that he was a "moderate". His master idea was to keep alive the spirit of moderation, and so prevent a vindictive peace that would merely sow the seeds of a Second World War. "If the spirit of moderation is not kept alive," he wrote, "the men in the trenches will have been betrayed, for the ensuing peace will never be the peace for which they have been fighting. Call no war successful until you have read the peace which ends it." Alas! the great majority of his contemporaries were obsessed by the idea of winning the war—somehow, anyhow, and could see no further than the day of military victory, and the supposed final crushing of German militarism. They were, in this matter, extremists, and wars are won by extremists, not by moderates!

A name prominently before the public at the beginning of the war was that of Sir Edward Grey, the Foreign Secretary. Sir Edward had occupied this office since the Liberals came into power in 1905. In 1906 he authorised British and French military officers to draw up plans to be put into operation in case of war with Germany. At the same time he emphasised that this did not necessarily commit Britain to fight. He was unpopular in Germany long before the war. He and King Edward VII were blamed for an alleged attempt to encircle Germany with a ring of hostile countries. His great hour came in the summer of 1914 —and he failed disastrously to avert the threatened war. Had he warned Germany in time that if she invaded Belgium Britain would fight with all her strength, the history of the world might have been very different. But Britain's ultimatum was delivered only when war had actually begun, and the German General Staff could assure the Kaiser that the hour was too late to alter their strategy. Grey's speech in the House on 3rd August excited general admiration, as he made clear that Britain could not stand aside if the neutrality of Belgium was violated. But Ramsay MacDonald wanted to know whether Britain's feelings would be the same had the French invaded Belgium, alleging that Grey had a secret understanding with France that we would fight if Germany attacked her, and that the invasion of Belgium was but the excuse. Grey continued at the Foreign Office until December, 1916, when he resigned along with Asquith. During that time he failed to enlist the support of Turkey, Greece and Bulgaria on the allied side. Italy joined the Allies, but according to Lloyd George, that was due to Asquith taking over the Foreign Office temporarily, while Grey was on holiday. Sir Edward was a dignified, reserved man, a "strong, silent man", some thought. More discerning observers noted his reluctance and lack of enterprise when a bold decision was needed. A business colleague said of him: "Grey is a good colleague, because he never takes any risks, and he is a thoroughly bad colleague for the same reason."

Although he was Foreign Secretary he knew little of foreigners and foreign lands. This may well explain his suggestion, in July, 1914, that a conference of all interested parties should be held in London, not in Paris, Berlin or Vienna, with a view to averting the threatened war. The interested parties ignored his suggestion. He was a gentleman and a patriot more than he was a statesman.

Sir Edward was succeeded at the Foreign Office by Arthur James Balfour, a Conservative. Balfour was Member of Parliament for the City of London, a former First Lord of the Treasury and leader of the House of Commons. In August, 1914, he offered his services in any capacity Mr. Asquith thought might help the war effort. He became First Lord of the Admiralty in the 1915 Coalition Government, and Foreign Secretary under Mr. Lloyd George. In the latter capacity he headed the British Mission to the U.S.A. in 1917. There he was hailed as "the most successful British envoy ever sent to the U.S.A." His name will always be remembered for the letter which became known as the Balfour Declaration, written on 2nd November, 1917. This letter to Lord Rothschild, Chairman of the British Zionist Federation, promised to seek the establishment of a national home for the Jews in Palestine. A lifelong bachelor, Balfour was also a man of great charm of manner, staunchly loyal to his friends, and possessed of great intellectual gifts.

These then, were chief among those on the Home Front who, in their strength, and sometimes in their weakness; in their wisdom, and sometimes in their foolishness; for they were but human, guided the destinies of the Empire until the long sought victory came at last to Britain and her Allies.

Chapter 13

ONWARD! CHRISTIAN SOLDIERS

IN common with the Government, and the country in general
the Church, in all her several denominations, was caught unprepared for the coming of a great war. The habit of churchgoing
was confined to a minority of the population, though to a larger
minority than in the second half of the twentieth century. The
decline in churchgoing had already set in since the turn of the
century. The advent of the bicycle, and now the motor bicycle
and car, provided many with an opportunity to escape from their
great grimy, smoky, ugly centres of population at the weekend.
Nevertheless, the Church still commanded the allegiance of a
large minority of the people.

The declaration of war presented the Church with a dilemma.
The neutrality of Belgium has been violated. Britain was faced
with the prospect of invasion by a ruthless foe. Should the Church
proclaim a crusade—a holy war—against the enemy? This
would imply that all the good was on one side, and all the evil on
the other. The Church was committed to preach the Gospel of
love and forgiveness. How then could she encourage British and
Allied Christians to slaughter German and Austrian Christians,
and later, Mohammedans from Turkey? Just how far could she
press the interests of the British Empire and her allies, and at
the same time commend the interests of the Kingdom of God?
In addition to all this, thoughtful people asked the Church to do
some explaining. If God was our "Almighty and most merciful
Father," why did He permit the war, and especially all the
125

innocent suffering it involved? On the other hand, the war
brought to the Church many opportunities to minister to those in
"trouble, sorrow, need, sickness or any other adversity."

The following extracts from a typical Church of England
parish magazine (that of Tamworth, Staffordshire), indicate the
guidance the Church tried to give to ordinary people in those
times.

> "Our conscience is clear on the justice and necessity of the
> war," wrote the Vicar. "It simply could not have been avoided
> and we feel confident that, by God's help, it will be brought
> to a successful issue."

That was written in August, 1914. In January, 1915, the Bishop
of the Diocese was writing:

> "We must not flinch from sacrifice, for there can be no peace
> until German aggression has been overthrown, and the demon
> of lust of power thrown out. Those who shirk now will be
> deservedly despised by all true Britons as long as they live."

In the following month some attempt was made to explain God's
action in permitting the war.

> "Why does God not prevent this sorrow and suffering? We,
> as a people, are becoming too selfish, and are neglecting the
> great object for which we were raised up in Europe, the ex-
> tension of the Kingdom of God, and the promotion of the
> well-being of the world."

There was no pretence that the war was a crusade, with all
the good on our side, and all the bad on the enemy side. "The
nation must awake to new life, and cast out the devils of intemperance and impurity," thundered the Bishop, in July, 1915. To
assist the casting out of these two particular devils women and

126

girls were advised to join the League of Honour, and thereby uphold the homes of our Empire by the practice of Prayer, Purity and Temperance.

This attitude of support for the war effort was continued throughout those years. "Shall not our single men be the first to offer themselves?" asked the Vicar, in support of the recruiting campaign. Later in the war people with high wages were urged to invest in War Loans, and so to help themselves as well as their country.

The signing of the Armistice was hailed as "The triumphant victory of Right over Might."

The man who was most successful in commending to ordinary people a God whom they could both love and respect in those terrible times was Geoffrey Anketell Studdert Kennedy. When war broke out he was Vicar of St. Paul's, Worcester. He would have liked to have joined up, as a chaplain, at once. But he felt that he could not so abruptly leave the parish to which he had come only three months previously. Opportunity for him to serve on the Home Front came immediately, when Worcester was made one of the training centres for Kitchener's new army. The Dean of Worcester, quick to realise Kennedy's ability as a preacher, invited him to preach to 2,000 men at the Sunday morning church parade in Worcester Cathedral. For the thoughtful ones in his congregation what he told them became a main topic of conversation during the coming week. Kennedy only joined the army when he was assured that proper provision had been made for the needs of St. Paul's parishioners. Not until December, 1915, did he arrive in France, where he became known as "Woodbine Willie", and the most famous of all the army padres. His unique appeal owed much to a combination of the mind of a scientist with the heart of a poet. He hated cant and hypocrisy, he spoke the language of the ordinary man, and his sense of humour was well developed. He presented to his hearers the image of a Christian minister as a courageous fighter, crusading among other things, for social justice.

127

One foggy evening in November, 1914, eleven people attended the induction service of Hugh Richard ("Dick") Lawrie Sheppard, in the Church of St. Martin-in-the- Fields, Trafalgar Square. In spite of poor health "Dick" Sheppard proceeded to make St. Martin's the church of the soldiers and the down-and-outs. Church and crypt were open day and night. In 1915 he began special Sunday afternoon services for men (and later women) in uniform, with a Guards' band to provide the music.

On two occasions the King, who was one of Sheppard's parishioners, was present. Soldiers direct from the leave train at Charing Cross, were often found in the congregation. Resting in a warm church sometimes sent them to sleep. Sheppard restrained zealous sidesmen from awakening them. "Broadminded Vicar advocates sleeping in church," reported the Press, approvingly. Among the laymen he welcomed to his pulpit, from time to time, were Lord Lansdowne and Edward Lyttelton, statesmen who suggested a negotiated peace rather than a fight to the finish. In addition to the shelter in the crypt for the homeless, Sheppard also sponsored a luncheon club for business girls and women, and a hostel for business girls from the provinces. He constantly urged his fellow Christians to carry their enthusiasm for Christian fellowship into those regions where there was much enthusiasm for fellowship, but not for Christianity. In later years, as a broadcaster and a pacifist, Sheppard became a national figure. During the war years he responded wholeheartedly to the spiritual hunger and the desire for help generated by the world conflict.

A future Archbishop of York, Cyril Forster Garbett, Vicar of Portsea, had on his staff of curates Philip Thomas Byard Clayton. Like Studdert Kennedy, he volunteered as an army chaplain. But the Army Chaplains' Department, like so many others, was caught unprepared, and without plans for the sudden expansion required. It was not until into 1915 that "Tubby", as he became universally known, found himself in France. There he gained lasting fame as the founder of Toc H.

128

Mention has already been made of Dr. Maude Royden and her anti-war views. In spite of these, and in spite of the fact that he was a woman and a communicant member of the Church of England, she was appointed Assistant Preacher at the City Temple in 1917. She retained this office until 1920. The City Temple was, and still is, the only Free Church in the square mile known as the City of London. Although Congregational in persuasion the City Temple has never restricted its pastorate to members of that denomination. The appointment of Dr. Royden by the broadminded Congregationalists caused a certain amount of confusion in some minds. The *Church Times* alluded to her as a Congregational minister, but Dr. Royden never asked nor desired ordination into the ministry of any Free Church. She believed that she had a vocation to the priesthood of the Church of England. But she was born too soon for her ever to realise this aim. When the error was pointed out the editor of the *Church Times* published a correction. "We apologise. Miss Royden is not a Congregational minister : she merely ministers in a Congregational chapel." Her views on the war were summed up in her widely read pamphlet, *The Great Adventure,* which advocated 'not peace at any price, but peace at any cost."[1]

In after years Dr. Royden was severely critical of much of the pacifism of the Great War period. She met much conceit, much bitterness, much imputing of wrong motives, and too often a purely negative attitude—don't fight—towards the war. Until one had a deep peace at the centre of one's being, she came to realise, one could not accept the hardship, and worse, that pacifism could involve, without bitterness and resentment. Long and hard training was required before one could lay down material weapons, and rely solely upon the power of the Spirit.

Canon Peter Green, who for so many years did outstanding work among the poor of Salford, was another who tried hard, in those perplexing times, to :

> Assert eternal Providence,
> And justify the ways of God to man.

129

9

A lifelong bachelor, he never took a single day's holiday durin
the whole course of the war. In 1917, when the submarine cam
paign threatened Britain with starvation, he preached a sermon
in Manchester Cathedral, on the text: "Blessed are the peace
makers." During the course of this sermon he told of a civilia
in a railway carriage, who asserted that the Germans were swine
and was promptly rebuked by a soldier. At a time when the pres
was carrying a number of reports of atrocities committed by th
Germans Canon Green carried out a personal enquiry amon
soldiers in Salford Royal Hospital, and among other of h
soldier contacts. Not a single one of these soldiers had actuall
witnessed any of these alleged atrocities, though they had hear
about them! For Canon Green, hatred of your fellows was a
ways of the Devil. He questioned the value of waging a wa
allegedly to end war if we were to be left with a legacy of mutua
hatred. Nor did the Canon agree with the view that German
was wholly responsible for the war. To blame Germany entirel
was to confuse the occasion of the war with the root causes. I
matters of self-interest, self-glorification and Jingoism German
did not stand alone. Therefore England, too, shared in the blam
for the coming of the world conflict. Throughout the war th
Canon maintained this distinctive note—the call for repentanc
—in his preaching, though it did not make for his popularit
among the ultra-patriotic, the-only-good-German-is-a-dead
German brigade!

The war also confronted the Salvation Army with accusation
of disloyalty. The Salvation Army was, and is, an internationa
organisation, trying to help all who are in need, regardless c
their nationality. During the war years the Army was well le
by General Bramwell Booth, the son of the Founder, Williar
Booth. In his New Year message, in the London *Times*, on 1s
January, 1915, he wrote: "I deplore the menace of bitternes
now growingly manifest in this country . . . Christ's prayer fo
His enemies was perhaps the highest of all heights to which praye
has led the human spirit, 'Father, forgive them, for they know

130

not what they do.' Can it not be our prayer, no matter to what nation we may belong?"

Strong meat indeed for a nation at war for its existence! Booth must be a pro-German to write such things at such a time! At the other end of the scale the Salvation Army was criticised by the pacifists for their evangelistic work among the troops, and for supplying ambulances, manned by Salvationists, to the Forces. But on other occasions, like that in December, 1917, when bombs on the Kings Cross area left 200 families homeless, no one criticised the actions of the Salvation Army. All concerned were relieved when Salvationists arrived at one o'clock in the morning, with travelling kitchens and other comforts. Early in the war Salvationists realised the plight of the soldiers waiting for hours on cold, draughty railway platforms, perhaps all night. Hostels were opened near railway termini, the first of them near Liverpool Street Station, where men might sup, and if necessary, sleep in comfort. A less popular activity was the regular visitation of German prisoners and interned civilians by Salvation Army officers. These, and other works of mercy, endeared the Salvation Army to the general public, even when General Booth wrote of sorrowing German homes as well as in British, and especially of a German mother who lost seven sons. The General also associated himself with the Archbishop of York in deploring the vulgar attacks on the Kaiser in certain newspapers. To those who looked askance at his seeming friendliness towards the Germans he replied that unless we could love our enemies, and forgive the injuries they did us, we were lost. "Christianity has never really been hurt by the war spirit," he wrote, "unless the war spirit has got into Christians themselves." The clue to understanding their wartime activities was: "Keep in mind that the Salvation Army is international—as Christ was."

The largest Free Church was the Wesleyan Methodists, 15 per cent of the soldiers registered their religion under that heading. Throughout the war years the Wesleyans maintained their large congregations in their Central Halls in London, and the provinces. Dr. Dinsdale T. Young continued to preach to crowded congregations in the new Central Hall at Westminster, and Dr. J. E. Rattenbury's sermons continued to attract the crowds to Kingsway Hall. Since 1907 the Wesleyans had held Sunday evening services at the Dome, Brighton. When this building was commandeered for hospital purposes, Sunday evening services were held in a local theatre When war commenced plans were in being for a new Central Hall, at Southall, with seating accommodation for 1,650 people, and for 1,000 Sunday School children. After negotiations the Government agreed to the work proceeding on the understanding that part of the rear premises would be used as a hostel for women munitions workers. The Wesleyans went further than this, and also provided a social club for the ladies. The premises were duly opened by the Lord Mayor of London on 11th October, 1916. "By faith the walls of Southall Mission were built in time of war and heavy taxation," jubilantly declared Dr. F. Luke Wiseman at the opening ceremony. The premises cost £25,000, and the first minister in charge was the Rev. John A. Broadbelt.

The Rev. Samuel Chadwick, who was elected President of the Wesleyan Conference in 1918, had many scathing things to say about war in general.

"War at its best is madness, and at its worst is hell let loose. It is irrational as well as wicked. To assume that grave questions can be settled by force is the height of absurdity. The assumption that might is right is a madness that begins by suspending the Ten Commandments. It settles nothing. The fighting leaves the question where it was, and when the guns are silenced the settlement has to begin, with the conditions anything but improved. War fever helps neither reason nor conscience. It may remove an awkward adversary, but to kill an opponent is no answer to his argument. To me it seems all so tragically wrong-headed, wrong-hearted, and wrong-principled. Both combatants sacrifice the nation's manhood and waste the nation's resources in an utterly senseless and wicked campaign of blood and treasure."

Hardly a recruiting speech, or wholehearted, unquestioning support for the war effort!

Mr. Chadwick sadly admitted that if sane people failed to settle their differences by mutual agreement, and appeal was made to force, no nation could give up its rights without a struggle and live. "Christianity does not sanction war," he pointed out, "but it has no power to prohibit the appeal to arms. War is unchristian because it is alien to the spirit and principles of the Kingdom of Christ, and only when the nations are Christianised will men learn war no more." In the meantime "tens of thousands of homes will be left desolate, and all for a quarrel in which they have no share, and for a policy which is part of a political game."

Mr. Chadwick's attitude to the war was typical of a great number of thoughtful people. Honestly unable to take the pacifist position, with extreme reluctance it resigned itself to what it felt was the slightly lesser evil of militarism.

The Primitive Methodists supplied 150,000 men to H. M. Forces. The first Primitive Methodist Conference after the outbreak of war, meeting at Reading in 1915, viewed "with grief and horror the European War, and regarded as guilty of treason those who provoked this awful conflict. . . ." They went on to assert: "We support His Majesty's Government in its call to Britain to spare neither blood nor treasure to crush the German conspiracy against the freedom and the peace of the world." The 1918 Primitive Methodist Conference placed on record its "admiration for the heroic sons of our Church who are engaged in deadly conflict with a ruthless enemy." One in ten of the 150,000 Primitive Methodist members of the Forces died on active service. Of them the Conference had this to say: "and having made the supreme sacrifice they are now assembled on the Plains of Peace, clothed in the white robes of immortality."

In 1914 the Primitive Methodists, along with the United

133

Methodists, the Baptists and the Congregationalists, were greatly concerned because they had no authorised chaplains either in the Army or the Navy. They confided their grievance to Lloyd George, who raised the matter with Kitchener. The War Minister referred to the four denominations contemptuously as "superfluous and eccentric sects" and suggested that they be continued to be classified as "Church of England." The four denominations refused to give way, and it was Kitchener who had to concede them their rights. The United Board was established, with Dr. J. H. Shakespeare, a leading Baptist, as its first chairman. Ministers of the four named denominations were then able to accept commissions as army or navy chaplains, and another small battle for religious liberty had been won. By the end of the war 218 chaplains had served under the auspices of the United Board. The Chaplain-General, the evangelical Bishop Taylor Smith, was in full sympathy with this decision.

A matter which stirred up much greater controversy was the question : "Shall the young clergy join up and fight the enemy like other young men?" Herbert Hensley Henson, Dean of Durham, well known for his recruiting speeches, was one who thought they should do so. The Bishop of Carlisle declared that he could find no reason, either in the New Testament or in the Canons of the Reformed Church, why the clergy should not be combatants. This view was shared by some serving soldiers, notably 2nd Lieutenant Donald Hankey, in his best-selling book, *A Student in Arms.* In the chapter headed "The Mobilisation of the Church", Hankey suggested the freeing of all the younger clergy for combatant service. In the life of the barrack room and the trenches, the young clerics, having learned about the faults, failings and virtues of the ordinary man, would be able to apply Christian doctrine to their situation, and learn to express those doctrines in language the ordinary man could understand. Hankey went on to suggest the closing down of much of the Church's parochial work for the duration of the war. Parochial work might suffer from the withdrawal of the younger

lergy, but the Church ought not to shrink from making the
sacrifice in view of the unique nature of the opportunity. If
necessary the retired clergy and all available women helpers
ould be mobilised, and the home parishes could sustain them-
elves until the end of the war. Then the younger clergy—those
who were still alive—would return with an appreciation of the
rdinary man's greatness in the trenches. Having broken down
he ordinary man's suspicion and envy of the parson's privileged
ot, they would be in a better position for the evangelisation of
he masses than ever before. Hankey's proposals included shut-
ing down perhaps a third of the city churches for the duration.
f the Bishops feared a shortage of clergy after the war, so many
having made the supreme sacrifice, many soldiers whom they
had influenced would offer themselves as candidates for the
priesthood.

A contrary view was set forth by some Army chaplains. Nine
of them, all former curates in the Parish of Portsea, signed a joint
letter to the *Church Times* and to *Challenge*. The letter, drafted
by "Tubby" Clayton, paid tribute to the heroism of those of the
younger clergy who remained at their posts, patiently and cour-
geously coping with the hardness of church work in the parishes.
They not only sustained the chaplains with their prayers, but
also moulded the younger generation on Christian lines, and
ministered to the increasing number of bereaved people. As a
tangible token of their regard for the clergy on the Home Front
the nine sent a cheque to the value of £200, for the fund to aug-
ment the stipends of underpaid curates. The views of the nine
chaplains were shared by the Archbishop of Canterbury, Dr.
Davidson. In spite of the eloquent pleading of some bishops, and
of the sincere and courageous Lieutenant Hankey, Dr. Davidson
said a firm "No" to the suggestion of making combatants of the
younger clergy. After careful consideration of the differing points
of view he announced his decision. He held to the conclusion
that the use of a rifle, bayonet or other offensive weapon was un-
fitting for a man in Holy Orders. He wrote:

135

"By every line of thought which I have pursued I am led to one conclusion . . . that the position of an actual combatant in the army is incompatible with the position of one who has sought and received Holy Orders . . . those who have been ordained to the Ministry of the Word and Sacraments ought even in time of actual warfare, to regard that Ministry whether at home or in the field, as their personal contribution to their country's service."

This ruling was generally accepted among the clergy as "Authoritative and eminently sensible." Very few clergy served as combatants. Others served with the Red Cross, accepting the Archbishop's ruling that:

"Provided a man can rightly leave his home, his work, I do not think that the fact that he is in Holy Orders ought in itself to be a bar to his undertaking work which is explicitly caring for the sick and wounded, and is distinctly non-combatant."

In 1916 the Church of England made a brave effort to rally Christian forces by launching a National Mission of Repentance and Hope. The war had produced a certain increase in churchgoing among those with near relatives at the Front. In some places prayer meetings were very well attended. Among the fervent supporters of the Mission was Canon Peter Green, whose constant war-time theme, as we have already noted, was Britain's need of repentance as well as Germany's. The feeling of optimism current in 1914 had evaporated, giving place to uncertainty and foreboding. Meetings were organised all over England, and among the soldiers in France and elsewhere. The mission was generally admitted a failure. Repentance was unpopular, and hope was confined to the personal safety of oneself and one's loved ones, to the prospect of a quick victory and an end to the fighting. Hensley Henson condemned the Mission for using nothing beyond conventional methods, "exhorting little companies of puzzled women," and with no vision of the larger teaching of the Church. Another severe critic was Mr. Horatio Bottomley, in his weekly *John Bull.* How dare the Church call our gallant lads to repentance? In his opinion all soldiers in those trying times were saints in no need of repentance. His bubble of pretence and unreality was promptly pricked by Studdert Kennedy. *"John Bull* says you're all saints," he told a crowd of soldiers. "Well, all I can say is: 'Eyes right,' and look at your neighbour."

The National Mission of Repentance was generally acknowledged to be a disappointment. There was no mass return to the Church. One type of church to report increased attendances during the war years was the Spiritualist, with its promise of communication with the dead. 1916, the year of the disappointing National Mission, was a good one for Spiritualist attendances. For that was the year of the Battle of the Somme, when 19,000 British soldiers died on the very first day of the slaughter.

A valuable piece of public service performed by the churches in the London area was described in a paperback, *Records of the Raids,* by the Bishop of Stepney. As the title indicates the book tells of the Church's efforts to succour the people, and to maintain their morale, at the time of enemy air raids. Church crypts were cleaned out, whitewashed, and fitted with seating accommodation. They made excellent air raid shelters, proof against anything but a direct hit. Some of these crypts were very large, providing safety for anything up to a thousand people.

A harmonium was often provided, and the time of danger was passed in hymn singing and prayer, interspersed by cups of hot cocoa provided by the church workers. Many people brought their own suppers to eat in comparative safety. If the church did not possess a crypt the walls and windows could be sandbagged, and again those who took shelter were safe from almost anything but a direct hit. Large vicarages sometimes possessed large cellars, and these again made good air raid shelters for as many as could be accommodated. Those clergy not occupied in leading hymn singing and prayers during the raids spent the time visiting sick and bedridden parishioners. Nor did they forget to visit underground stations also used as air raid shelters. The times were very demanding on many of the clergy, strained as they often were by the loss of a curate who had joined up as an army or navy chaplain. When people emerged from the shelter provided by the Church they sometimes found their homes destroyed by the raiders. To provide against this eventuality parish rooms and institutes were opened as temporary homes, complete with beds and other furniture. Children suffering from shock were sent into the country for a fortnight. Scouts and members of the Boys' Brigade and the Church Lads' Brigade acted as messengers, gave warning to "Take cover" when a raid was imminent, and sounded the "All clear" when the raid was over. They made themselves useful, too, after raids, by searching for missing members of families. Evidence was not lacking to show that this kind of witness was more effective than the kind of witness embodied in the National Mission of Repentance and Hope. A north London vicar, when the "All clear" was sounded, watched the crowd pouring out of his crypt. A big, burly fellow turned to him and said : "I've said a lot of hard and bitter things about the Church in my time, but I shall have to shut my mouth after this. I can't think ill of the place that befriends and shelters me." Francis Lloyd, Lieutenant-General, Commanding London District, praised "the wonderful working Clergy of all denominations" who have so unostentatiously helped in these terrible times by relieving the destitute, ministering to the suffering and infusing courage and cheerfulness among those who are targets of the murderers who invade the heavens during the periods of the air raids." The provinces, too, suffered from air raids, and the Church rendered similar service as in London. Hull was a favourite target of the bombers. When a bomb landed on a row of small houses two small boys were blown out of bed, and found

138

hemselves in the street wearing nothing but shirt neckband and
vristbands, and as black as coal all over. They were taken to the
earby Thornton Hall Wesleyan Mission. The minister, the Rev.
3. H. Hulbert, bathed them in the copper in the mission kitchen.
Next day Hull was talking about "the parson that bathed the
ids," with a consequent increase in respect for the Church.

An example of undenominational evangelistic and social work
among both sailors and soldiers was the Royal Sailors' Rests at
'ortsmouth and Devonport, a work started in the latter part of
he nineteenth century by Miss Agnes Weston. Originally in-
ended for sailors only, the centres were opened to soldiers also
vhen war came. Here men could write home, play games, chat
vith friends, and listen to, or take part in, music and singing.
Coffee, tea, buns, books and paper were available, and family
prayers, at which attendance was voluntary. Similar facilities
were offered by the Y.M.C.A. in centres in various parts of the
country. When the Crystal Palace was taken over by the Naval
Battalion, for training purposes, Miss Weston and her helpers
co-operated with the Y.M.C.A., to minister to the needs of the
5,000 men under the great glass roof. As opportunity offered,
Miss Weston urged sailors to join the Royal Naval Christian
Union, the Royal Naval Temperance Society and the Alliance
of Honour. Miss Weston also organised a band of ladies to knit
warm clothing for blue jackets patrolling the North Sea, "where
the north east wind shaves you for nothing," as one sailor ruefully
observed. Soldiers in the trenches also benefited from the efforts
of the same ladies. In addition to all these services Miss Weston
was responsible for sending nearly 100 tons of magazines, book-
lets, New Testaments and Gospels to serving sailors and soldiers.
A capable public speaker, Miss Weston on one occasion addressed
1,600 men at the Crystal Palace. Such was the effect of her ora-
tory that a new branch of the Royal Naval Temperance Society,
300 strong, was there and then launched.

So the Church "soldiered on" through the dark years. Her
theological colleges were closed, and taken over for hospital and

139

other wartime purposes. Some theological students became com-batants, and others joined the Royal Army Medical Corps. Some tutors became chaplains, and others went into parish or circuit work. Add to this the natural wastage of clergy through death and retirement, combined with the number who became army or navy chaplains (over 3,000 in the Church of England alone). By 1918 the Church's resources were severely strained.

As the months and years went by the real issues of the war became clearer. Increasingly the Church criticised war hate and the demand for reprisals. Speaking about the increasing hatred of Germany Dr. John Clifford, the Free Church leader, said : "I have no doubt we shall win the war, but I sadly fear that we shall lose the peace." He had condemned the Boer War, but supported the Great War, when little Belgium had been out-raged. He thought that Britain must resist oppression, as he had done all his life. After a heavy daylight raid on London, in 1917, the Bishop of London rebuked those who called for reprisals in kind against the German murderers of babies. He felt that the mourners would not wish to kill 16 German babies, in revenge for the 16 English babies who perished in the raid.

What would Jesus do in this situation? Where would He be now? A great many people asked these questions. Chaplain Neville Talbot felt that Christ, had He been then walking the earth, would have been a stretcher-bearer, truly in the army and of the men. Others struggled towards the view that Christ was above the struggle, sitting in judgment upon all—aggressors, defenders, neutral. Allied and Central Powers alike had, by their former way of life involved all in this way of life which was the opposite of all Christ taught and practised. The function of the Church was to present Him as both in, and above, the struggle, calling mankind to turn to a higher manner of life, without which there was no hope for the glorious future this war was supposed to bring.

Chapter 14

PACK UP YOUR TROUBLES AND . . . SMILE!

"IF you can't learn to make jokes, you'll drown in the tears," Lloyd George once told a friend who was going through a difficult time. In a later war one Mona Lott was famed for her assertion: "It's being so cheerful that keeps me going." The wartime padre, Studdert Kennedy, in his book, *Food for the Fed-up*, pointed out that fed-up people, either soldiers or civilians, could have no hope of victory, since they lacked the will to win. 'The fed-up spirit is the soldier's greatest enemy," he warned. The same truth applies to the civilian, without whose support the army and navy would quickly cease to function. It was therefore essential that civilians be kept reasonably cheerful, in spite of food shortages, long working hours, and all the other sorrows, dangers and inconveniences of war. One of the most popular wartime songs expressed this truth in homely and topical terms:

> Pack up your troubles in your old kit bag
> And smile, smile, smile.
> While you've a lucifer to light your fag,
> Smile boys, that's the style.
> What's the use of worrying?
> It never was worth while.
> So, pack up your troubles in your old kit bag,
> And smile, smile, smile.

Somehow the sorely tried British public did manage to kee
reasonably cheerful, and the national morale was sustained unt
victory came. They did make their jokes, and they did keep o
smiling, in spite of all their wartime trials. That national inst
tution, *Punch,* which maintained its pre-war price of 3d. unt
1917, then raised it to 6d., gave a good lead in the matter o
keeping people cheerful.

Wryly humorous comments on food shortages were a peren
nial theme in the pages of wartime *Punch.* The coming of foo
rationing, with its attendant allotment of coupons, inspired
drawing of a nurse announcing an addition to the family to
boy of about ten years. "There's a little baby brother come t
live with you," she says. "Well, he can't stay unless he's brough
his coupons," is the reply.

The quality of meat available provoked a drawing of a fami
dining on shepherd's pie. "Mother, *must* I eat this?", plaintive
asks the son of the house, and explains : "It's such a particular
nasty bit of the shepherd." The butter shortage is reflected in
joke about two waitresses gossiping about one of their colleagues
"She's a clever one," says the first waitress. "Yes," replies h
companion, "She knows which side her bread's margarined."

Allied to food shortages were rising prices. A small boy is pi
tured with his mother in a grocer's shop. He displays much i
terest in the shopman's explanation of the high price of egg
"But, Mummy," he exclaims, "How do the hens know we're
war with Germany?"

On the subject of women leaving their homes to do war wor
an extract from a schoolgirl's essay on "Women's work in wa
time" is quoted. "Women are now driving tram cars instead
their husbands."

Punch contrived to find humour even in air raids. One draw
ing was captioned : "A use for Zeppelins." It portrayed a ma
who had lost his latchkey standing outside his house, which ha
been damaged in a Zeppelin raid. Not only the windows, b
also the front door, had been blown in. Surveying the spa

where the door had been, the keyless one exclaims: "Hello! Here's a bit of luck!"

By January, 1918, British aircraft had begun to raid German towns, to the alarmed surprise and horror of the German people. A *Punch* cartoon entitled "An easy conundrum", portrayed two stout, heavily moustached Germans staring horrified at the ruins of bombed buildings. "These accursed British, our so peaceful and cultured Mannheim to bomb!" says one. "What devil taught them this frightfulness?" asks his amazed companion.

That the ordinary person's sense of humour was still very much alive is suggested in the picture of a stout housewife hanging out newly washed white sheets to dry. A genial old gentleman, passing by, remarks: "Washing day, I presume." "Ho no, sir! We're expecting an air raid, and we're all going to surrender!"

The wounded soldier, who had received a "Blighty one", was regularly portrayed as still able to joke. An old lady asks one such: "How did it happen?" "It was a shell, Mum," replied the wounded one. "A shell! O dear! Did it explode?" "Explode, mum? Not likely! It just crept softly up behind me—and bit me."

Another wounded soldier, when asked: "How did you get that wound?" answered: "I was leaning up against a barrage, thoughtless like, when it lifted, and I fell into the trench."

By these, and countless other witty and humorous items, *Punch* made its own unique contribution to the maintenance of the national morale, and thus to the winning of the war.

Turning to real life, instances of cheerfulness under trials are plentiful. In some instances the humour was unconscious on the part of the speakers but it helped to cheer up someone else. One old lady in the much bombed East End of London recounted how, during a raid, she stood with her son in the small hall of her house, and "saw the front door go right past us up the staircase." Another exclaimed indignantly of the Zeppelins: "I don't think they ought to be allowed to make them things, and go up there, prying into the Almighty's private affairs." Yet another East End

143

lady, who was in her backyard when she sighted a Zeppelin overhead, said: "So I ran into my kitchen, and in a minute or two looked out of the front door, and blest if it wasn't waiting for me there! I don't call it natural!"

Some old ladies were afraid to retire to their beds at night, for fear of being caught at a disadvantage during a raid. In the autumn of 1918, as the prospect of victory grew brighter, people began to discuss how they would celebrate the coming of peace. "Well, I know what I shall do," said one old East End woman, "I shall take me stockings off. I 'aven't 'ad them off for two years."

The drive for recruits in the earlier years of the war, before the coming of conscription, also had its lighter moments. One recruiting poster displayed a smart young British soldier standing on the French coast, reaching across the Channel to a reluctant civilian. "Come, lad! Lend us a hand!" ran the caption underneath. Some wag added this advice: "Don't be so daft, mate. Stay where you are."

A leading literary figure of the day was the poet, novelist and wit, Gilbert Keith Chesterton. He was forty years of age in 1914, and his figure was distinctly paunchy. He was medically rejected for every form of war service, even that of special constable. During the course of a recruiting speech he was delivering a woman in the audience rudely interrupted him with the pertinent question: "Why aren't you out at the front?" G.K.C. gazed down at his bulging waistcoat, and replied: "If you will step round to the side, madam, you will see that I am."

Mr. Lloyd George, on occasion, could produce lighthearted remarks about the general situation. Commenting on Winston Churchill's obvious readiness, even eagerness, to get to grips with the enemy, he said: "Winston reminds me of a dog sitting on the Dogger Bank, with his tail between his legs, looking at the rat who has just poked his nose out of the hole on the other side of the water."

One Sunday afternoon a number of wounded soldiers in

Charing Cross Hospital were observed throwing pennies out of the window, to a Salvation Army band playing hymns in the street outside. The matron questioned whether they could really afford to throw away so many pennies out of their slender pay. 'As a matter of fact," one soldier explained to her, "We had a bet on who'd be the first to throw a penny down the big brass trumpet."

So the British public contrived to find some humour in the trials they underwent in the war years. The present generation may turn up its nose at the unsophisticated, even corny, humour of these years. But the jokes and the wit served their purpose. The people kept their sense of humour. Morale was sustained, and the war was seen through to victory.

10

Chapter 15

ARMISTICE

THE year 1918 dawned on a war weary, sorrowing, apprehensiv
British public. The collapse of Russia had enabled Germany to
transfer a large number of troops to the Western Front. Tha
meant Germany was in a favourable position to launch an all
out effort on the Western Front to finish the war in her favour
The knowledgeable ones predicted victory for the Allies in 1919
at the earliest. The expected German attack came on 21st March
and very soon it was a case of "backs to the wall" for the Allies
For the first time since 1914 German armies again directl
threatened Paris. The German "Big Bertha" guns actually shelle
Paris, from a range of 75 miles. In the beginning the war ha
been a crusade, a stern duty that no honourable man could avoid
By 1918 we were just fighting a war, whose end was not yet i
sight. The great and high aims with which the conflict began
the rights of small nations like gallant little Belgium, and th
advancement of democracy, were almost forgotten.

To add to the trials of the times a new pestilence appeared t
scourge mankind. Popularly known as "Spanish influenza", i
was prevalent all over Europe, U.S.A., India and Australia. Th
world was taken by surprise by this deadly new strain of influ
enza virus. The influenza was followed by pneumonia. In Eng
land the epidemic began in mid-June, in Lancashire and York
shire. Soon deaths in London alone averaged over 1,000 weekly

Few British families entirely escaped the ravages of the disease, and by May, 1919, the total of British dead reached 200,000. In the world at large the death roll was estimated at a minimum of 15 millions.

As we have mentioned in a previous chapter, August 31st, 1918, was the occasion of the one day strike of the London policemen. That was the day when "This country was nearer Bolshevism than at any time," according to Lloyd George.

But by this time the news from the battlefronts was distinctly more encouraging. The German attack, after its initial success, had exhausted itself. The field grey tide began to recede. August 8th was acknowledged by the German High Command as the Black Day of the German Army, when they were defeated at Amiens. The German retreat began and continued through the late summer and autumn. Her allies sued for peace—first Bulgaria, then Turkey, then Austria, and lastly Germany herself. With growing relief the British people, in the early days of November, read newspaper headlines like:

END OF THE HOHENZOLLERNS
KAISER ABDICATES
CROWN PRINCE ALSO GOES
REVOLUTION ALL OVER GERMANY

As the autumn leaves fell from the trees, and the prospects of peace by the end of the year grew daily brighter, the politicians began to prepare for an early election. Labour Members prepared to withdraw from the Coalition as soon as hostilities ceased, and to fight the election as a separate Party. As the war drew to its close they prepared for the new era soon to dawn. There was to be no patching up of the old economic order. They thought out telling slogans like: "A Peace of Reconciliation", "Hands off Democracy!", "Land for the Workers", "A Million Good Homes" and "A Levy on Capital". They discussed and clarified their post-war aims and demands — the immediate nationalisation

147

of the mines, railways, shipping, armaments and electric power; the abolition of unemployment; the legal limitation of hours of work; the drastic amendment of acts dealing with factory conditions, safety and workingmen's compensation. Their political opponents were also busy, thinking up slogans like: "Hang the Kaiser!", "Make Germany Pay!", "Squeeze Germany till the pips squeak!", "They'll deceive you yet, those Germans!", "Homes fit for Heroes!" and "A Land fit for Heroes to live in".

Monday, 11th November, 1918, dawned grey, but clear. The Armistice ("a suspension of hostilities, a truce by mutual agreement between the belligerents"), was duly signed, and came into force at 11 o'clock on that morning, when firing ceased on the entire front. In London, Big Ben, which had struck the fateful hour of 11 p.m., announcing the outbreak of war on Tuesday, 4th August, 1914, now struck 11 a.m., to announce the end of that same war. The prophets of gloom had been confounded in their dismal predictions of a war dragging on possibly until 1920. Maroons, the signal for the end of an air raid, were sounded, and works buzzers, railway engine whistles and steamboat sirens joined in the gleeful cacophony which broke out all over the country. Peoples crowded into the streets from their places of work, and everywhere there were scenes of jubilant relief. Winston Churchill stood at the window of the Hotel Metropole, waiting to hear Big Ben's chimes. From all sides people streamed into the streets, church bells rang and "burdens were lifted" from a sorely troubled people. No sooner had Winston entered his car, to drive to the House of Commons, than twenty people climbed on it, and they made their way down Whitehall amid a cheering, shouting multitude. On the Stock Exchange the members sang the *Old Hundredth* and *God save the King*. General Bramwell Booth, the head of the Salvation Army, was at his home, at Hadley Wood, when he heard the news of the Armistice by telephone. He ordered the Staff Band to march to the Mansion House, where they led a crowd estimated at 30,000,

148

n the singing of the Doxology. Later in the day General Booth spoke from a window at the Salvation Army headquarters in Queen Victoria Street, calling upon all to honour God, and to remember His mercy to the nation.

At Buckingham Palace the King, the Queen and Princess Mary appeared on the balcony. A Guards Band played *Rule, Britannia, Home, sweet home, Tipperary, Land of Hope and Glory* and the *Marseillaise,* the huge crowd who had gathered joining in. For the Royal Family the war ended as it began, with a shouting, jubilant crowd in front of the Palace.

In provincial centres the same kind of scenes were enacted. The streets were filled with people drunk with thankfulness and relief. "Everyone wanted to kiss somebody!" said the Rev. Samuel Chadwick, President of the Wesleyan Conference, describing the spirit abroad. People gathered at their Town Halls to hear the Mayor make an official announcement of the signing of the Armistice. In at least one instance a Mayor reminded his hearers that this was an armistice, and not necessarily peace. Events were to prove the Mayor of Widnes all too correct, for it was a twenty years armistice he announced on that dull November morning. In some places an attempt was made to get drunk on something more substantial than thankfulness and relief. Public houses were broken into, and the small stocks of beer consumed. In other places buses and trams were seized, and made to career round the streets, crammed with flag waving, singing, shouting people.

But some were unable to join in the general rejoicing. Many a widow, and many a mother bereft of her sons, sat mute that day. The *Daily Express* reported a working class woman rushing into the rejoicing crowd in the Strand, bursting into tears, and exclaiming: "O, my poor boy," until willing helpers took her gently away. Sir Henry Wood suggested going out and joining in the general rejoicing, but Lady Wood considered this "a vulgar idea." So the Woods celebrated the coming of victory with a high tea of boiled eggs. In the House of Commons that afternoon,

149

immediately after prayers, Mr. Lloyd George rose to announce the signing of the Armistice. He then read its terms. These were severe, and the thirty-five Clauses were designed to prevent Germany from resuming hostilities however much she disagreed with the terms of the Peace Treaties yet to be drawn up. Typical Clauses enacted that Germany should immediately evacuate all the invaded countries: Belgium, France, Luxemburg, and Alsace-Lorraine too, which territory Germany had taken from France after the Franco-Prussian War of 1870-71. Germany was to hand over, in good condition, 2,500 heavy guns, 2,500 field guns, 25,000 machine guns, 3,000 trench mortars and 1,700 aeroplanes (both fighters and bombers). All German submarines were to be surrendered forthwith, and the German navy was to be interned under British supervision. All Allied prisoners, but not German, were to be repatriated. The Allies were to occupy all territory west of the Rhine, including the bridgeheads on the right bank. The Allied blockade of Germany was to continue. As Mr. Lloyd George read on through the formidable list of Armistice terms, even the greatest Hun haters must have felt a glow of satisfaction. Imperial Germany was down, out and rendered harmless for the foreseeable future.

Mr. Lloyd George concluded: "At 11 o'clock this morning came to an end the cruellist and most terrible war that has ever scourged mankind, I hope we may say that thus, this fateful morning, came to an end all wars. This is no time for words. Our hearts are too full of gratitude to which no tongue can give adequate expression. I will therefore move that this House do immediately adjourn, until this time tomorrow, and that we proceed, as a House of Commons, to St. Margaret's, to give humble and reverent thanks for the deliverance of the world from its great peril."

Mr. Asquith then spoke, expressing his agreement, and his satisfaction that the terms of the Armistice made it quite clear that the War really was at an end, since Germany was deprived of the power to resume it. The motion was adopted, and, in the words of *Hansard* : "Whereupon Mr. Speaker and the Members proceeded to the Church of St. Margaret, Westminster, and with the House of Lords, attended a Service of Thanksgiving to Almighty God, on the conclusion of the Armistice signed today."

Moved by a similar spirit of gratitude and relief that the dark nightmare had ended at last, all over the country people gathered in their churches. There preachers reminded them that even the most powerful cannot trifle with the moral government of the world. One set of tremendous problems had come to an end, to be replaced by another—the problems of peace, reconciliation and reconstruction. But the story of how the British people tackled the host of new problems left behind by the War is outside the scope of this work. We merely note their menacing existence, awaiting the attention of the shouting, cheering Armistice crowds.

Chapter 16

THE REAL BLIGHTY

To the soldier in the trenches "dear old Blighty" seemed a Paradise. "A Blighty one", a wound sufficiently bad to ensure the sufferer being sent back to England, was something greatly desired. The soldier on active service compared his lot with that of the civilian back in England. The soldier, with his slender Army pay, was daily subject to strict discipline. He faced death and discomfort twenty-four hours a day. He felt a certain sympathy towards the enemy, who was in a similar plight, and referred to him as Jerry. Any disobedience, anything approaching the nature of a strike on the part of the soldier, would be dealt with by a firing squad. Uprooted from his former settled, if drab, form of life, the soldier longed ardently for Blighty. He envied the civilian his domestic comforts, his opportunity to earn big wages or make large profits, his personal freedom. The civilian, who often referred to the Germans as Huns, neither saw nor knew the grim realities of war. The soldier not only saw them face to face, but had to carry out the grisly and highly perilous business of twentieth century warfare. Yet many a soldier's last memories of Blighty were not particularly happy ones. He, a civilised young man, had spent months learning to form fours, and to bayonet a sack of straw, so that he might kill civilised young men from the other side of the North Sea. During the period of training many had been fortunate to lodge in civilian billets. But others had memories of bedraggled tents on waterlogged turf, where men caught pneumonia and died in dozens, until the War Office awoke to their plight, and arranged civilian billets. The civilian was, of course, immeasurably better off than the man in khaki in the Flanders mud. But Blighty, on closer investigation, was a long, long way from Paradise.

Back in Blighty the civilian was never in danger of forgetting the war. He was subjected to an unprecedented stream of propaganda by posters, which confronted him on every hoarding in almost every street. Until the coming of conscription many posters were produced by the Parliamentary Recruiting Committee, representative of all three political parties. Party organisation was harnessed to the business of recruiting. Local party helpers distributed posters, and also delivered circulars to electors, asking them to come forward as recruits when called to do so by the War Office. The famous Kitchener poster was the first of many.

December, 1914, brought a poster showing a smiling, pipe-smoking soldier saying cheerily: "Come along, boys!" The bottom part of the poster contained an extract from a letter written in the trenches of the Aisne by General Sir Horace Smith-Dorrien: "The moment the order came to go forward there were smiling faces everywhere." In view of this the reader was exhorted to ENLIST TODAY.

Another early poster depicted a man in civilian clothes watching a column of soldiers go marching past. 'Don't stand looking at this," he was brusquely told, "Go and help." Other posters called in the aid of feminine influence. A white haired old lady said sternly to a hesitating young man: "Go! It's your duty, lad." In another a group of women resolutely declared: "Women of Britain say GO."

Later came the grim words: "Another call! More men, and still more, until the enemy is crushed." Another famous poster looked beyond the end of the war when, thanks to the men who had volunteered for war service, victory had been won and peace restored. A well dressed, prosperous looking man in his thirties was depicted with an ashamed look on his handsome face when his children asked him : "Daddy, what did you do in the Great War?"

With the coming of conscription the poster campaigns switched to other aspects of the war effort. The call was transferred from men to women, and the vital part they must play if the war was to be won. Women were needed both in the factories and on the land. One poster pictured two women at a factory bench, and underneath were the words : "These women are doing their bit. Learn to make munitions." A poster calling for recruits to the Women's Land Army carried the slogan : "God speed the plough, and the woman who drives it too." Another series of posters appealed to civilians to use their money to support the war effort, by investing in the current War Loan. One such carried a large reproduction of a five shilling piece, supported by the legend : "War Loan. Invest 5/- and help your country." Newspapers, too, regularly printed appeals and advice on how the civilian could help to win the war. "Hide the poker" ran one such, pointing out the waste of fuel involved in the homely custom of poking the domestic fire. With radio and television still in the future the Government, through the then existing media, made notable advances in the art of moulding public opinion.

The necessities of war vastly increased the power of the State in other ways, notably in industry. For the successful prosecution of the war the State took up itself the right to control, direct, divert or restrict any industry, if the national interest called for such action. Hundreds of factories and workshops were commandeered by the State, though their ownership and management remained unchanged. Railways and shipping were likewise brought under State control. The means of production and distribution were left in their owners' hands, but only so long as they conformed to the demands of the State. The State also set up new factories and workshops, where thousands were employed producing war materials. For the hundreds of thousands of working men and women Blighty was long hours of arduous, often dangerous, work, linked with a struggle to keep wages at

east abreast of rising prices. Blighty was drunkenness reaching
dangerous proportions at Gretna and other large munitions
centres, and Liverpool dockers wrecking public houses in protest
at watery beer rising to the unprecedented price of 8d. per pint.
Throughout the war years the State kept a firm hand on industry,
sometimes calling would-be strikers to heel by the by no means
idle threat of conscripting them into the army.

This great increase in the power of Government was reflected
in other directions—in the introduction of conscription, in the
rationing of food, and in the drastic control of the manufacture
and sale of intoxicants.

In his leisure hours, as we have noted, the average civilian,
deprived of football matches, which were suspended for the duration, wanted light, frothy entertainment. Nothing serious, and
demanding concentrated thought, was required. Middle-aged
and older people, who also were comfortably off financially, were
not unduly disturbed by the exigencies of the times. A reading
of the Journals of Arnold Bennett, for instance, suggests that. for
some, the war had comparatively little effect on their comfortable
existences.

But for the many the war was supremely a time of great
anxiety and, all too often, of great grief, even though Britain
lost less than the other great Powers in life and material destruction. Russia lost 1,700,000 men, Germany 1,600,000, France
1,400,000 killed, and the United Kingdom (as distinct from the
Empire), approximately 740,000. If the Black Day of the German army was 8th August, 1918, the British army's Black Day
was 1st July, 1916, the first day of the Battle of the Somme.
19,000 British soldiers died on that day, the greatest loss ever
sustained by the British army on one day. Blighty was a place of
grief for rich and poor, for Prime Minister Asquith, in London's
West End (whose first born son Raymond was killed at Ginchie,
leading his men), to the dwellers in London's East End. The
Rev. C. W. Lyndall, nephew of Lord French, the leader of the
British Expeditionary Force in 1914, was killed at the Battle of

Jutland, on the eve of his wedding. Of forty-four boys who entered Sherborne School in 1911, only half of them lived to celebrate their fortieth birthday. 5,688 ex-Eton boys served in the
Forces. 1,469 were wounded, and 1,159 were killed. "Life's fair
adventure scarcely yet begun," as one of their memorials so poig-
nantly expresses this tragedy.

A photograph wreathed in black ribbon or paper, or if no
photograph was available a black wreath or bow, was to be seen
in the window of many a home where a loved one was lost.
Blighty was crowds of callers at the Admiralty, after the Battle
of Jutland, mainly women seeking news of their loved ones engaged in the battle. One woman, unable to obtain information
about her husband and three sons, all serving in the Royal Navy,
appealed indiscriminately to others in the crowd, and to passers
by as to what she should do. Blighty was the mother of Jack
Cornwell, the boy hero of Jutland, arriving too late at Grimsby
hospital to hear the last words of her son : "I know Mother is
coming. Give her my love."

In some families the son, or husband died, shot not by the
enemy, but by his own countrymen, for cowardice, desertion or
looting. Sylvia Pankhurst knew one such family in the East End
of London. Their son enlisted in September, 1914, at the age of
18. In April, 1916, after one month in the firing line, he broke
down and fled. He was caught, convicted, and shot for desertion. Miss Pankhurst's representations to the War Office resulted
in the family being informed that their son "died of wounds."
But other families, in a similar plight, had no Sylvia to plead for
them. Apart from the slaughter at the front death took its natural
toll of great and small during those war years. The year 1915
saw the passing of W. G. Grace, the famous Gloucestershire
cricketer, at the age of 67. The Champion, the Doctor, the Old
Man, or W.G., as he was variously called, scored 54,000 runs
including 126 centuries, before his career in first class cricket
ended in 1900. As a bowler he took over 2,800 wickets, and in
seven seasons scored over 1,000 runs and took over 100 wickets

William Willett, the Farnham builder, died in that same year. For years he had been campaigning for clocks to be advanced one hour in springtime, and put back one hour in the autumn, in order to make the best use of daylight. He died in March, 1915, thus not living to see the Daylight Saving Bill become law fourteen months later. As might be expected his revolutionary proposal that during a defined period legal time should be one hour ahead of Greenwich Mean Time, met with widespread opposition. One who thought daylight saving a good idea was Winston Churchill, but a great war was necessary to make people generally to realise that the idea was sound and sensible. In that same month there also died the great Jewish financier and philanthropist, Sir Nathan Meyer Rothschild. At the time of his death he was looked upon as the world leader of the Jews. He was also president of the British Red Cross Society.

The well known actor-manager, Sir Herbert Beerbohm Tree, died on 2nd July, 1917. He achieved wide fame, not only as an actor in Shakespearian and other plays, but also as the organiser of Shakespearian festivals at the Haymarket.

Three weeks before the signing of the Armistice Dame Agnes Weston, the Sailors' Friend, founder of the Sailors' Rests at Devonport and Portsmouth, mentioned in an earlier chapter, died at the age of 78. She was buried with full naval honours, a hitherto unprecedented thing for a woman.

Henry James, the American novelist who became a naturalsed British subject in 1915, died less than a year later. As a novelist he excelled in drawing a contrast between the new civilisation of America and the old civilisation of Europe. He was more interested in portraying character rather than in incident. He had lived in Europe since 1869, mainly at Rye, in Sussex, and in London, where he died at Chelsea. Among his forty odd novels and his hundred short stories he is remembered today for his ghost story *The Turn of the Screw*, and for his exquisite *Portrait of a Lady*, which was serialised on television over fifty years after his death. In 1914 he began writing two novels, *The*

157

Ivory Tower and *The Sense of the Past,* which remained un-
finished at his death. His ardent sympathy for the British cause
led to his naturalisation in the second year of the war.

Among the eminent Churchmen who died during the war
years was the theologian and Bible scholar James Denney, principal of Glasgow Free Church College, whose book on the
Atonement had attracted wide attention during the pre-war
years. He died on 15th June, 1917. Henry Scott Holland, Canon
of St. Paul's Cathedral and Divinity Professor at Christ Church
Oxford, philosopher and theologian, who died in March, 1918
took a great interest in social work at Poplar and Bethnal Green
He gave much thought to the bearing of Christian principles on
economic problems. One who knew him well described him as
"a great and forceful wind sweeping through Anglicanism, in
vigorating, freshening quickening all it touched." A lover of
peace who was a victim of war was James Hope Moulton, Wesleyan minister and a specialist of international fame in two subjects, New Testament Greek and Zoroastrianism. Overseas
missions and the amelioration of social conditions in Britain
were two other great concerns of his. In 1917 he journeyed to
India to lecture on Zoroastrianism to the Parsees. On the return
journey the boat on which he was travelling was torpedoed in
the Mediterranean Sea. He and others were placed in a small
boat. Though worn out by weariness and exposure, he kept on
rowing until his strength failed him. In his last hours he ministered
to dying Lascars until death claimed him too.

Blighty also meant the civilian in many parts of the country
confronted with the grim reminders of the conflict overseas, in
the form of grievously maimed and wounded soldiers, dressed
in their hospital blue uniforms. An observer at Brighton, in the
later days of the war, commented on the hundreds of wounded
men to be seen. Many were on crutches, bereft of a leg. Others
had an arm missing. Passers-by, hardened to the grim scene
hardly gave them a passing glance. Londoners became familiar
with the nightly line of ambulances at Charing Cross Station

collecting the wounded, the fortunates with the "Blighty ones", and taking them to hospital.

The Church finished the war weaker numerically, and profoundly shaken by events. She was much the weaker because she faced the post-war years bereft of so many young and enthusiastic young men who would have been the leaders, if death had not claimed them on Flanders fields and elsewhere. She would miss, too, the many thousands of men who had been effectively broken of their habit of churchgoing by army and navy service. Some, who had been regular churchgoers before 1914, now looked askance at a Church which had appealed to God for victory in the name of the gentle and peaceful Jesus, had issued pulpit appeals for cannon fodder, and prayed consistently for the speedy overthrow of the enemy, with all the pain and bloodshed this entailed. John Galsworthy, from his Devonshire retreat, wrote: "If this war is not the death of Christianity, it will be odd. We need a creed that really applies humanism to life." Others saw the war as a blow to the old denominational spirit, which exalted one's own sect above all others as the way to heaven. In his presidential address to the 1918 Wesleyan Conference at Manchester the Rev. Samuel Chadwick declared: "The Church has been judged. It has been weighed in the balances and found wanting. In the trenches they have discovered the futility and folly of our divisions. What we want is a revival of religion." This does not imply that the prophetic word was always missing, as we have noted in the chapter on the war and the Church. Reflecting upon the Armistice the *Methodist Recorder* exhorted its readers "not to be German in the nature of the triumph, but to wish Germany well, and not let her starve. The best reply to Germany is to be as much unlike her as possible, and not vengeful."

One bright feature of those dark years was the growth of the spirit of brotherhood. Men sank their petty disputes, even their party politics, and combined, as never before, against the common enemy. The words of Francis Drake, uttered concerning

his world voyage of 1577-80, came true again on a scale tha
would have astounded him. "I must have the gentlemen to hau
with the mariners, and the mariners with the gentlemen. Let u
show ourselves to be of one company." That spirit was very mucl
alive during the war years. The presence of a common dange
and a common sorrow inspired teamwork on an unprecedentec
scale. The coming of peace unfortunately dissipated much o
that spirit. Nevertheless the war demonstrated that no task is too
great, no expenditure too high, if the people will co-operate to
carry it out. The spirit of the people was demonstrated by ever
air raid. Resentment at lives lost and material damage done wa
of material help to the recruiting campaign. Terrorism was ex
posed as a futile weapon against a spirited people. Indignan
resolve to prosecute the war against the terrorists far outweighe
any panicstricken appeal for peace at any price. In this war, fo
the first time, the whole population was not only involved, bu
was regarded by the enemy as a legitimate object of destruction
to be bombed, shelled and starved into surrender. In the peril
and hardships and sorrows of wartime Britain many discovere
a comradeship and a purpose in life they had never known be
fore—and which they lost when the war ended. For wome
generally the war was a time of progress towards a greater free
dom. They not only gained the right to vote, but were also de
livered from bondage to large hats, masses of hair and long
trailing skirts!

As a result of their wartime activities many women also los
their inhibitions about swearing, smoking, drinking in pubs an
using cosmetics. As we noted, in an earlier chapter, war was th
great liberator of women, as well as the great destroyer of mer

In the realm of politics the great wartime casualty was th
Liberal Party. In the years before the war their prestige wa
great and their future seemed secure. Had they not curtailed th
power of the House of Lords, and introduced beneficial measure
like social insurance and old age pensions? Their leader, Asquitl
was an intellectual, and a man of great integrity. But Asquit

160

was less successful as a wartime leader. When he was replaced by Lloyd George, in 1916, the Party was split. In 1914, as a united Party, with a fine record of social reform, they were the recognised alternative to the Conservatives. By 1918 the shape of British politics showed signs of radical alteration. For many years to come the once great Liberal Party was to be a spent force in British politics. Their place as the alternative to the Conservatives was to be taken by the Labour Party. Yet Ramsay MacDonald, the Labour leader, perhaps the worst hated man in the country in 1918, was at the lowest ebb of his fortunes at the time of the signing of the Armistice. Lloyd George, his leadership crowned with victory, was second to none in public esteem and prestige. Five years later Ramsay MacDonald was Prime Minister, though admittedly dependent upon Liberal support.

The war shattered the simple faith of those who still believed in the inevitability of human progress, "stage by stage to the Golden Age," in the words of the hymnwriter Walter Hawkins. Those who pinned their hopes of no more war to the international solidarity of the working classes were also rudely shocked. Solidarity there was, but it was restricted to the section of the working class on each side of the conflict. Progress there was in those war years, especially in the increasing efficiency of the means of destruction. Great strides were made in the development of the internal combustion engine, basis of the armoured car, the tank and the fighting and bombing aeroplanes. Civilian and commercial interests were later to benefit from this progress. When war began aeroplane flights across the English Channel were commonplace. When the war ended aeroplane engines had been developed which would soon be flying, not just across the English Channel, but across the Atlantic Ocean. Human progress in those war years was especially noticeable in the scientific and technological realms. Progress was also made in dealing with one of Britain's greatest social problems, that of drunkenness. Army service not only broke some of the good habit of churchgoing on Sunday, it also broke others of the bad habit of getting drunk, or at least fuddled, every Saturday night. Light ales and short[e] periods of opening had a similar beneficial effect on workers o[n] the home front. Their wives and families also reaped the benefi[t] of these changed habits. The benefits to the public generally [of] the drastically reduced number of opening hours were recognise[d] and made a permanent feature of national life.

"And what good came of it at last?" asked little Peterki[n] concerning the Battle of Blenheim, in Southey's poem. For th[e] Allies the Great War was also a famous victory. But the Bligh[ty] to which the surviving soldiers were to return was, in the wor[ds] of Lloyd George: "a sorry prize for so much blood and sweat[,] even allowing for the fact that victory meant twenty years respi[te] from "the German menace".

A young man who managed to join up in 1914, although h[e] was then only sixteen years old, who spent most of his time i[n] Blighty training men for the battle front, wrote: "We were th[e] ones who lost our youth. We went into the army as carefree boy[s] and came out hard and cynical, with the minds almost of middl[e] aged men." Others, whose loved ones had perished in the hol[o]caust, found adjustment to the new order very difficult. Cynth[ia] Asquith wrote: "One will have to look at long vistas again. On[e] will at last fully recognise that the dead are not only dead for th[e] duration of the war."

The Blighty of 1918 was a very different place to the Bligh[ty] of 1914. Along with fallen sons, husbands and sweethearts ma[ny] old inhibitions and customs had been swept away. Organis[ed] labour was more determined than ever to gain its fair share [of] the national wealth. The prevailing Armistice mood of gratitu[de] and relief was destined to be short lived, as the grim realities [of] peacetime revealed themselves.

However, let a lady, Nancy Astor, have the last word abo[ut] life in Blighty from 1914-18. In 1951, having experienced tw[o] world wars, and remembering the terrible air raids of the Seco[nd] World War, Lady Astor said of the first war: "Looking ba[ck] over it, it was a very quiet sort of war."

BIBLIOGRAPHY

War Memoirs of David Lloyd George. (Odhams).
Our Own Times. Stephen King-Hall (Nicholson & Watson).
History of Europe. H. A. L. Fisher (Arnold).
The Home Fronts. John Williams (Constable).
English History, 1914-45. A. J. P. Taylor (Clarendon Press).
The Twelve Days. G. M. Thomson (Hutchinson).
Post-war History of the British Working Class. A. Hutt (Gollancz).
The Common People. Cole and Postgate (Methuen).
History of Widnes. G. E. Diggle (Corporation of Widnes).
Strikes. R. & E. Frow & M. Katanka (Knight).
Conscience and Politics. John Rae (Oxford University Press).
Objection Overruled. David Boulton (MacGibbon & Kee).
Records of the Raids. H. L. Paget (S.P.C.K.)
Newspapers of the First World War (David and Charles).
Punch, 1914-18.
St. Editha's, Tamworth, *Parish Magazine,* 1914-18.
Queen Mary. Pope-Henessey (Allen and Unwin).
Kitchener. Philip Magnus (John Murray).
Beaverbrook. Peter Howard (Hutchinson).
James Ramsay MacDonald. Lord Elton (Collins).
Bramwell Booth. C. B. Booth (Rich and Cowan).
Asquith. Roy Jenkins (Collins).

163

Wearing Spurs. John Reith (Hutchinson).
Nancy. Christopher Sykes (Hutchinson).
My Eighty Years. Robert Blatchford (Cassell).
Canon Peter Green. H. E. Shean (Hodder).
The Years of Promise. Cecil Roberts (Hodder).
H. R. L. Sheppard. R. Ellis Roberts (John Murray).
Sir Henry Wood. Reginald Pound (Cassell).
Sir Edward Marshall Hall. E. Marjoribanks (Gollancz).
My Life among the Blue Jackets. Agnes Weston (Nisbet).
Olave Baden-Powell. E. K. Wade (Hodder).
Women on the Warpath. David Mitchell (Cape).
The War to end War. H. G. Wells (Palmer).
Personal Knowledge.

INDEX

165

HISTORY OF THE AMATEUR THEATRE

GEORGE TAYLOR

This book is the first to deal exclusively with the amateur theatre which has an important place in the cultural and social life of the community.

It traces its history from the birth of drama in Greece to the origins of amateur theatre in this country during the middle ages. Its development from the mystery plays of the tradesmen's guilds through the morality plays and interludes to the amateurs in Shakespeare's day.

The author shows how the rising of standards by dedicated individuals at the beginning of the twentieth century was followed by an amateur dramatic renaissance after World War I which continued until World War II during which the amateur theatre played its part in keeping up public morale.

Following the war, government and municipal support is noted with the development of theatre in education and the formation of civic theatres, the financial help through Regional Arts Association, and recognition by television and radio.

Illustrated with several unique and historic photographs.

ISBN 0 85475 125 4   Illustrated.

DORSET THROUGH HISTORY

PETA WHALEY

A very interesting and easily read book which has chapters on many famous people and events and landmarks which have made the history of Dorset.

These include Alfred the Great, Edward the Martyr, Sherborne and Sir Walter Raleigh, Corfe Castle and Lady Bankes, Charles II, Monmouth, Judge Jefferies and the Bloody Assizes, William Wordsworth, Nelson's Hardy. The Tolpuddle Martyrs, William Barnes the poet, Thomas Hardy the novelist and Lawrence of Arabia the campaigner.

Illustrated by several photographs which makes the volume a must for all lovers of Dorset.

ISBN 0 85475 11 0   Illustrated.